# The Indian War Diar

# We Were Not Summer Soldiers:

## f Plympton J. Kelly
## 1855~1856

With

Introductory Essay and Annotations

by

William N. Bischoff, S.J.

*wm n. Bischoff, SJ.*

TACOMA
Washington State Historical Society
1976

Printed by
Craftsman Press
Seattle, Washington
U.S.A.

*Dedicated to*

MERV, JOE, ANTHONY, ROSEMARY
AND BETTY

*My very special brothers
and sisters*

Plympton J. Kelly.

# Preface

This modest contribution to the sources of western history has been in the making for 20 years. A crowded teaching and administrative schedule explains part of the delay. The greater hindrance to rapid completion was the more unusual circumstance of the diary being in two widely separated notebooks: one in the Beinecke Rare Book and Manuscript Library, Yale University, New Haven, Connecticut; the other in the Oregon Historical Society Library in the Oregon Historical Center, Portland, Oregon; with neither knowing of the missing portion of its manuscript. The problem was compounded by the first part of the diary, November 22, 1855 to March 16, 1856, being erroneously attributed to Kimball B. Mercer. Despite remarkable assistance from Mrs. Mabel Schendal, Hillsboro, Oregon, a descendant of Kimball Mercer, four years of diligent searching failed to uncover sufficient material for the briefest biography of the alleged author and forced a review of the entire project.

The reassessment of past work brought me back to the Oregon Historical Society Library where the second portion of the manuscript had been recently deposited and correctly ascribed to Plympton J. Kelly. The diary is reunited in this edition, after several decades of separation, thanks to the unselfish cooperation of two notable libraries.

A book is usually the result of the coordinated efforts of the writer and a multitude of assistants. The list of helpers is long on this present trek from brave beginning to relieved finish. There is no practical way of pursuing prolonged research on a topic with widely scattered sources without repeated recourse to unmet aides willing to help slake one's thirst for the facts. Some 200 queries directed to county clerks, probate courts, local newspapers, libraries, historical societies

7

and individuals from London to Los Angeles, with few exceptions, received gracious and expert attention.

Most of the research for this book was done during an uninterrupted year in the rich collections and superb facilities of the Oregon Historical Society. Mrs. Jean Brownell, Mrs. Ernest Elkins, Mr. Richard Engeman, Mr. Robert Fessenden, Miss Priscilla Knuth, Mr. Millard McClung, Miss Jeannette Stewart and Mr. Thomas Vaughan, director, have my unreserved gratitude for manifest competence generously shared.

The notes make clear the extent of my indebtedness to other libraries and depositories, with their dedicated staffs. Mr. Willard Ireland, archivist, Provincial Archives, British Columbia, lightens any work day with his readiness to smooth the researcher's path. Besides the incomparable thrill of pouring over manuscript treasures, there are warm memories of lunch in the Henry E. Huntington Library cafeteria with fellow students from the earth's corners and learned, sophisticated, engagingly relaxed members of the library administration and staff. Puckish John E. Pomfret, director, and Ray Billington, senior research fellow, spent lunchtime formulating strategy for the spirited lawnbowling that filled out the noon hour. Some acquaintanceships begun in hallowed corridors and around worn tables have grown into precious friendships.

Wherever the search took me, selfless staff members of each institution recorded in the notes readily shared their knowledge and the resources in their charge. My thanks are genuine for the help of: Miss Mary Johnson and Mrs. George Gilbert, Spokane Public Library; Miss A. M. Johnson, Hudson's Bay Company Archives, London; Miss Haydee Noya, the Huntington Library; Mr. Archibald Hanna, The Beinecke Rare Book and Manuscript Library, Yale University; Mr. David C. Duniway and Mr. James D. Porter, Oregon State Archives; Mr. Martin Schmitt, University of Oregon Library; Mrs. Hazel E. Mills, Washington State Library; Mr. Frank Green, Librarian, Washington State Historical Society; Mr. Robert Monroe and the late Charles M. Gates, University of Washington. No less grateful am I to the devoted staffs of the Bancroft Library, Berkeley; Manuscript Division, Library of Congress; Maryland Historical Society, Baltimore; and the National Archives, Washington, D.C.

Permission to publish excerpts from varied manuscript and printed sources has been granted by the Provincial Archives, British Columbia, Victoria, B.C.; Fort Vancouver Historical Society, Vancouver, Washington; Hudson's Bay Company, London; Henry E. Huntington Library and Art Gallery, San Marino, California; Oregon State Archives, Salem; Oregon Historical Society, Portland; University of Oregon Library, Eugene; *Pacific Northwest Quarterly* (University of Washington); Polk County Historical Society, Dallas, Oregon; Spokane Public Library, Spokane, Washington; University of Washington Library, Seattle; and The Beinecke Rare Book and Manuscript Library, Yale University, New Haven, Connecticut.

I appreciate especially Dr. Clyde Patton's excellent map done with the uncalculating generosity typical of real scholars.

There are others to whom I am thankful for their confidence in this project. Reverend John J. Kelley, S.J., my religious Superior at the beginning, freed me from other duties to permit full time concentration on the book. The Religious of the Good Shepherd at Villa St. Rose, Portland, made the year easier by providing pleasant surroundings for living and writing. My lamented mentor, critic, and friend, the late Reverend W. Lyle Davis, S.J., encouraged and prodded when quiescent inactivity was a more attractive path, a role assumed in more recent times by Mr. Robert Hitchman with my sincere appreciation. The concluding weeks of this venture have been greatly brightened by my association with Mr. Nurmi Hansen and Howard Vierling whose unfailing courtesy cloaks their formidable grasp of the art and craft of book-making. Mr. and Mrs. James Brown, Jr., Mr. and Mrs. Lawrence V. Brown, Rev. and Mrs. Charles Schreiner, and Dr. and Mrs. Robert Swart with their timely non-academic support elicit my particular grateful acknowledgment.

Whatever of merit is in these pages is freely shared with every active helper in the enterprise; while all deficiencies belong to me.

WILLIAM N. BISCHOFF, S.J.

# Table of contents

# Illustrations

# Maps

# Introductory essay

About ten o'clock in the morning on a cold, rainy September 25th, 1855, Andrew J. Bolon overtook a small party of The Dalles-bound Yakima Indians in the Simcoe Mountains. The tall, red-bearded Indian sub-agent quietly shared his lunch with them and then, while warming his hands at the fire, his feet were jerked from under him, two Indians jumped on his arms, and Stah-kin slashed his throat. They buried him beneath a pine tree, before shooting and burning his horse.[1] Two nights later a Yakima woman reported the slaying to Nathan Olney at The Dalles[2] where rumored hostilities were in the air, and the news was printed in Portland for all to read on Saturday, September 29th.[3]

Major Granville Haller's two hastily readied U.S. infantry companies left Fort Dalles October 3. A week later these badly bloodied avengers dragged themselves back to their post. Major Gabriel Rains marshalled U.S. forces at Fort Vancouver and asked Oregon's Governor Curry to enroll four volunteer companies to comprise a certainly successful punitive thrust. Curry's call for eight, not four, volunteer units reflects the prevailing hysterical reaction to a threat of undetermined gravity. Why so many people were startled by this Indian outburst is puzzling, when mounting evidence of a long-festering enmity was apparent at every turn!

The sub-agent's murder was not the inexorable result of cynical, greedy, cheating whites relentlessly pushing fiercely determined natives. There was more to the racial rancor in Oregon and Washington territories, 1855-1856, than Indian stubbornness and white exploitation. Both parties were victims of an inability to adjust to an opposing mode of life. Seeds of disaster often were not deliberately sown by evil white men as much as they accidentally fell onto fertile soil

15

through a failure to grasp or refusal to accept the Indian's concept of the possession and use of land so totally different from that cherished by the white men.

The vast area, for which blood would flow, was the unfenced homeland of a dozen nomadic tribes long before the coming of the whites. The tribes lived along the streams in fishing season, in the mountains at berry-ripening time, and in the valleys when roots and greens were ready. Their home was a region over which they roamed freely in gathering their food and choosing the more salubrious camp sites for the various seasons of the year.[4] They had no fixed abode on a restricted plot of ground nor would they live by repeatedly wounding Mother Earth with systematic plowing, planting and harvesting.

The first whites in the Oregon Country caused no spontaneous explosion between the races. There was a half century of considerable commercial traffic with the interior tribes of both territories. Fur traders built Fort Okanagan at the confluence of the Okanagan and Columbia rivers in 1811. This post was followed by Fort Walla Walla, 1818; Fort Colville and Fort Vancouver, 1825; and Fort Nisqually, 1832. The Hudson's Bay Company traded in this entire area for more than three decades without a single Indian uprising of any moment. Fur men, it is true, were basically transients bent upon business with no thought of changing the living patterns they found. They generated little or no friction for they did not covet the Indians' lands; they encouraged the natives to trap and hunt while constituting no threat to traditional mores.

Even this scene remained mostly untouched by the occasional venturesome emigrant to the Far West up to the early 1830s. Their small number and scattered cabins caused no genuine concern to the unmolested Indians. The primitive innocence of these vast western reaches was violated, however, before the close of the decade, by forces loosed far from the unspoiled forests and plains. By the early 1840s Oregon changed from another vague and distant "garden," long disputed with the British, into an immediate goal.

These new migrants, a thousand in 1843, came not for God, not for furs, but for land upon which to raise a family. They came looking for fields where Indians had roamed since time before memory. These trespassing newcomers, from an antagonistic culture, would destroy native life unless hurled back. In terms of new diseases, the whites destroyed it innocently enough; in terms of threatened and persistent infringement on land, of road builders, game hunters, farmers, whiskey traders and irresponsible miners — a general pushing around of

16

those previous masters of what they surveyed — created an explosive situation.

Steadily mounting numbers on the road to Oregon, three thousand in 1845 with tempting herds, were matched by more raids, more ambushes, and more killings along the way. Accumulated wrongs and brooding suspicions, blazed in deadly anger at Marcus Whitman's Waiilatpu Mission, near Walla Walla, Nov. 29, 1847. The violent massacre of Whitman, Narcissa, his wife, and twelve others was the beginning of the Cayuse War, 1847-1848. Before hastily gathered white volunteers and a peace commission reached hostile country for either talks or battle, Peter Skene Ogden of the Hudson's Bay Company negotiated the release of the captured survivors. In 1850, the five alleged murderers were surrendered, tried and hanged according to white man's law.

Passage of the Donation Act, Sept. 27, 1850, promised since 1838 in various "Oregon" bills before Congress, speeded the decline of Indian-White relations by the invitation it provided for greater numbers of settlers. Every white settler or occupant of the public lands, including American halfbreeds over 18 years of age, a citizen of the United States, or having declared his intention of becoming such, or who made such a declaration on or before Dec. 1, 1851, then residing in the territory, or becoming a resident before December 1850, was granted 640 acres, if married, half of which would belong to his wife in her own right, and 320 acres to a single man, or if he marry within a year from Dec. 1, 1850, 320 more for his wife, no patents to be issued until after four years' residence.[5] Hence a person satisfying these conditions could claim lands under a law not recognized by the Indians. This absence of any agreement by the natives to dispose of their title to the lands heightened an already ominous situation.

Attempts were made to negotiate peaceful cessions of lands claimed by various tribes in western Oregon and Washington. Three commissioners, John P. Gaines, Alonzo A. Skinner and Beverly S. Allen, were named in 1850 to arrange treaties with the tribes in Oregon. They concluded six agreements with Willamette Valley tribes in the spring of 1851 before news arrived that Congress had dissolved all special Indian commissions and provided for a Superintendent of Indian Affairs.[6]

The efforts continued under Anson Dart, Superintendent of Indian Affairs for Oregon, who concluded 13 pacts with as many tribes in western Oregon Territory by November 1851. These agreements, involving some six million acres west of the Cascades, and an earlier separate one signed with the Rogue River people in June 1851,

17

totalled 20, all of which were unratified, as yet, by the United States Senate.

Formal discussion with the Yakima, Cayuse, Umatilla, Nez Perce and other interior tribes awaited the establishment of Washington Territory, March 2, 1853, and the return of its first governor, Isaac I. Stevens, from Washington, D.C., December 1854. His instructions as Superintendent of Indian Affairs envisaged the uniting of all tribes in his jurisdiction under the terms of six or eight treaties. This utopian scheme ignored real differences rooted in language, custom, habits and ancient rivalries. A white man's lack of understanding did not transmute incompatible natives into gentle neighbors.

Energetic Governor Stevens, in the flush of transcontinental railroad exploration and envisioned settlers, began talking with Indians in western Washington Territory, December 1854. An agreement with the Nisqually, Puyallup and other tribes was signed at Medicine Creek, Dec. 26, 1854. There followed, in rapid succession, treaties with Duwamish, Suquamish and others signed at Point Elliott, Jan. 22, 1855; with the S'Klallam, Sko-ko-mish and neighboring bands concluded at Point No Point, Jan. 26, 1855; and with the Makah at Neah Bay, Jan. 31, 1855.[7]

Joel Palmer, Superintendent of Indian Affairs in Oregon, expended matching effort on the Willamette tribes. The Kalapuya, Molalla, Yamhill and others entered into a pact Jan. 22, 1855, the very day Stevens' sessions at Point Elliott were finished. The treaties with the Willamette Valley natives and with the Nisqually were the only ones ratified by the U.S. Senate March 3, 1855, and proclaimed April 10, 1855.[8]

Before meeting the increasingly sullen interior tribes, Stevens sent his talented young secretary, James Doty, as an assiduous advance agent of the projected talks. Doty's repeated visits to the Yakima, Walla Walla, Nez Perce and adjacent peoples were marked by patient explanations and tireless striving to engender greater receptivity toward the impending council. People whom he did not visit were invited to confer with him. He sent these invitations and announcements as far north as the Hudson's Bay Company's Fort Colville and as far east as the Bitterroot mountains. His travels and letters were largely responsible for the enormous gathering of natives, commissioners, interpreters, missionaries, soldiers and assorted personnel that met at the Walla Walla council grounds "six miles from Way-lat-poo on the Mill Fork of the Walla Walla," May 28, 1855.[9] Some 900 Nez Perces, 300 Cayuse and most of the 600 Walla Walla attended the opening deliberations on that warm, dusty Monday

*Ou-hi. Chief of the Yakima Indians.*

morning. Kamiakin, Owhi and Skloom, Yakima chiefs delayed by the high water, joined the parley late the next morning.

Stevens' unflagging drive for acceptable agreements went on for two weeks of fatiguing speeches under scorching skies. He sought to consolidate on one reservation the Okanagan, Colville, Yakima, Klickitat and Columbia River bands as far as the Cowlitz. Another reserve was planned for the Walla Walla, Cayuse and Umatilla. Besides land, the amount and schedule of compensation were meticulously outlined.[10]

Throughout the proceedings the Yakima were wary until "all possible influences were made to operate upon them" on June 8 "& a bargain was made." The agreement and all prospects of any accord were very nearly shattered at the next day's meeting when Looking Glass, a Nez Perce just back from buffalo hunting, caustically assaulted the proposed surrender of tribal soil. Nothing was signed at the close of this day's stormy exchanges.[11]

Despondent frustration turned into suspicious gratification that evening in Stevens' tent whither came Kamiakin, and those linked with him, asking to sign the treaty. It was nothing more, in reality, than a follow-up to Kamiakin's talk with Stevens that morning in which he expressed weariness with the talks and his willingness to sign the papers so he could go home. Many of the whites interpreted his theatrical nocturnal acquiescence as the easiest way of gaining time in which to prepare for war.[12]

Whatever lay hidden in the restless future was of slight moment when ranged alongside the real gain of 16,920 square miles comprising some twenty-two million acres of ceded land. Pre-treaty settlers would now rest more easily on their possessions. The U.S. Senate did not ratify the pact until March 8, 1859, with the obvious consequence of the Indians receiving nothing for what they had given up.[13] One wonders whether events would have been altered by the Indians clearly understanding the legal necessity of ratification. Certainly Stevens let himself think that peace would now prevail. He insisted in his subsequent speech to the Volunteers that he left Walla Walla Valley June 16, 1855, for the Blackfoot Council "little thinking that those who had promised to be faithful to me would be up in arms against the whites."[14]

Perhaps this avowed confidence was sincere. Probably, too, the Indians did prepare for war during the summer months. The certainty is that within a week of Stevens' departure from the Walla Walla treaty grounds, newspapers reported the ominous presence of gold at the mouth of the Pend Oreille River, some thirty miles north of Fort

Colville. Four men were back from the new strike with three pounds of dust worth $16.75 per ounce. Others were making from $10 to $30 a day with only the simplest equipment.[15]

This stirring news of gold shared the same issue with news of the treaties with the tribes beyond the Cascade Mountains. Vic Trevitt, The Dalles merchant, spread the word that these tribes had ceded to the U.S. Government the Touchet, Walla Walla or Whitman Valley, that of the Tucannon, Grand Ronde prairie and the Umatilla Valley below McKay's — "A country equal, it is said, to the whole Willamette Valley, both in extent and quality of soil." Gold and land distributed without a ratified treaty was an eight-word tragedy.

Each week throughout the summer the treaties' full texts appeared as legal notices in the newspapers, along with seductive accounts of the new mining area. Forty or fifty men reportedly left French Prairie late in June, 1855, bound for the gold fields. A week later readers received careful directions about the best route to the mines, a forthright reminder that low water made August and September the best months for working the deposits and a tempting miner's story of several pounds of gold dust sold to the Hudson's Bay Company.[16]

High water, hostile Indians and barren country did not slow the constant, even daily, departures of large parties in search of gold. No one was immune from the gold infection. Some public officials, the word was, resigned their offices to join the crowd.[17] Hundreds from Oregon and Washington, as well as from more distant places, were hurrying to the mines by September 1855. The fever lessened slightly in early fall as a result of more temperate reports by disappointed or dispassionate observers. More restrained appraisals, however, did not shrink significantly the numbers rushing to the mines.[18]

Collisions were almost inevitable between the lengthening lines of searchers and the increasingly resentful Indians already weighing the possibility of exterminating the trespassers. Earlier intimations of grave trouble were ignored. In July, the very month after the Walla Walla Council, it was acknowledged "that a portion of the Indians are dissatisfied with the late treaties . . .; and declare that they will not abide by said treaties, and that the whites shall not settle upon the lands acquired by the United States." Some returned prospectors warned of imminent war; and others insisted that "the Indians are perfectly friendly."[19] Events resolved the divergent views sooner than anticipated.

The pace to disaster was quickened by the murder of a miner on the Pend Oreille River September 1855. Three additional killings, that of Henry Mattice on the trail to Seattle, and the ambush of Walker* and

Jamison* while crossing the Cascade Mountains September 14, were ill omens. The peril did not diminish because Mattice was allegedly killed for assaulting the daughter of Teias, a Yakima chief. Perhaps his being better known in Olympia explains why Mattice's murder ignited the tinder into flames of war.

Charles Mason, acting governor during Stevens' absence at the Blackfoot Council, asked Major Gabriel Rains, commander at Fort Vancouver, to send a detachment of U.S. troops to apprehend the murderers, punish the guilty, discover any unreported killings and protect travelers still on the trails.[20] Two days later, September 24, he made an identical request of Captain Maurice Maloney, commander at Fort Steilacoom.

Far on the opposite edge of Washington Territory, the news of Mattice's death came to the knowledgeable ears of Andrew J. Bolon while the sub-agent was visiting the Spokane Indians. He hurried to The Dalles where he stayed briefly before starting to St. Joseph's Mission among the Yakimas. There he hoped to question Owhi, the Yakima chief, about the murder. Bolon spent only two hours at the Mission on Sunday afternoon, September 23, because Owhi was not there. Whether darkness, weariness or weather kept him from arriving at The Dalles on Monday, September 24, remains unknown. After lunch on Tuesday he was standing by the fire warming his hands when Stah-kin lunged at his throat. The long summer was ended.[21]

Rumor and fact were indistinguishable to whites frantically set upon revenge and protection from what was conceived as a "general Indian uprising" from Southern Oregon to Puget Sound. Bolon was killed, according to news accounts, because hereafter the Indians would "kill friend and foe alike, that they regarded all whites their foes." A report of 500 tribesmen assembled within fifteen miles of White Salmon added to the fright. And even more alarming was information "that the Kaiuse, Walla Wallas, Peluce, Snakes and a large portion of the Deschutes Indians are now holding a council high up on & East of the Deschutes River for war purposes . . . and that they intended . . . to attact the Dalls kill the inhabitants & burne the place & for this latter object they are making arrangements." There was widespread talk that the Yakima chiefs were persuading, cajoling and threatening other tribes into joining "in a general rising against the Americans." Into this arena of fear and hatred the punitive force thrust northward from Fort Dalles.[22]

Major Granville Haller set out, Oct. 3, 1855, with a total command of 106 to redeem the white man's honor and punish the guilty. That night at their first camp, Old Yice, a paid Indian spy, warned them of

22

FORT VANCOUVER, W. T.

*Fort Vancouver, W.T., 1853.*

an immense number of "warriors collected together in the Yakima Valley." He vigorously advised an immediate return to The Dalles for reinforcements because "it would be out of the power of the soldiers, with double their present force, to escape destruction, if they once encountered Kamiakin's warriors." His absolute refusal to accompany the troops further into Yakima country underscored the sincerity of his counsel.[23]

Nothing daunted, but with sharpened alertness, the army advanced until it clashed with the Indians at Toppenish Creek on the afternoon of October 6. A round or two from the howitzer, plus a frontal assault before dark, flushed the natives from the bush-lined opposite bank. The soldiers took up their night vigil, "without food or water or grass," but with one comrade dead, two gravely, four seriously, and two slightly wounded.[24]

The beleaguered command watched with impotent concern as the enemy force grew and inched closer throughout the next day. A few Indians were killed as Haller's untested recruits consumed ammunition in firing "eternally without aim or mark." An estimated thousand fighters surrounded the exposed camp until almost sunset, October 7, when they loosened their tight encirclement.

23

This momentary respite afforded a chance of retreat to the weary, parched and hungry defenders. Their withdrawal went undetected until the rear guard became separated from the main body on the unfamiliar, black-shrouded terrain. The two segments were not reunited until the next afternoon.

Once discovered, the withdrawal quickly became a running battle in which the retreating men were slowed by their wounded and further handicapped by inferior arms, jaded animals, and near total personal exhaustion. Taunting Indians tried to burn them out with grass fires that counter fires neutralized. Stalking foes mercilessly harrassed the troops from thick smoke cover effected by creeping pine needle fires. Finally, a bold charge into the sheltered woods startled the lurking natives into headlong flight and allowed the dragging regulars to reach Fort Dalles without additional fighting.[25]

The beaten column had buried four comrades in the Indian country, brought with them the body of another and counted seventeen wounded among the survivors. Not only were the warring tribes unbowed and unbeaten, but their confidence was greatly enhanced. News of the defeat excited immediate concern for safeguarding against Indian attack rather than restoring white prestige. Any ultimate white victory was of little solace to those staring at possible death.

The mauling dealt to Haller's men loosed a torrent of terror-inspired activity. Volunteers were recruited, the country scoured for arms, blockhouses built in many places, people crowded into towns and forts, and business paralyzed by rumors and reports of families butchered in their cabins. Many settlements west of the Cascade Mountains became armed camps patrolled by jittery civilian soldiers.[26]

Reaction to the Indian success was equally rapid, strenuous and disorganized (according to some critics) among civil and military officials. Hurried measures aimed at quick punishment of the tribes were announced, Oct. 9, 1855, the very day on which Lt. Edward Day left Fort Dalles with 50 men to escort Haller's riddled ranks to safety.[27] Major Rains at Fort Vancouver declared that "the whole force of the District will be immediately called into the field to meet and subdue the foe."[28] He asked Governor Curry for four companies of volunteers to bolster a force inadequate "to subdue these Indians, the Yakimas, Klickitats, and maybe some other bands." Volunteers were sought, also, from Charles Mason, Washington Territory's acting governor.[29]

Emergency efforts originally aimed at helping Haller, once he was safe, were directed toward the mobilization of a certainly successful

24

*Columbia River immediately below The Cascades.*

force against the arrogant enemy. Major Rains toiled painstakingly before finally leading 365 officers and men from Fort Dalles, Oct. 31, 1855.[30]

The opening day or two of the campaign were notable only for the piercing cold weather. On the third day, however, two bold Indians swept through camp and drove off 25 horses and five mules. Lt. Phil Sheridan pursued them hotly but in vain. The thieves did unintentionally reveal two large caches of dried salmon, tools, hatchets and similar supplies. The army took or destroyed everything they found as dim consolation for the Indians' humiliating raid.[31]

Governor Curry's response to Rains' appeal for volunteer forces was energetically effective, if not deliberate and neatly efficient. His proclamation, Oct. 11, 1855, called for eight companies of mounted volunteers, each with one captain, one first lieutenant, one second lieutenant, four sergeants, four corporals and 60 privates. Enrolling officers were designated for each county and the troops were to rendezvous without delay opposite Portland on the east bank of the Willamette River.[32]

Stiff criticism, then and later, was leveled at practically every facet of the organizing of the Oregon Mounted Volunteers.[33] All was done simultaneously; troops signed up, horses found, clothes, tents, food, forage, guns, powder, lead and everything an army needs were purchased in a matter of days. Some sheer chaos, considerable wastage, widespread inflationary profiteering, and not a little plain, old-fashioned speculation characterized portions of the enterprise. Yet, two days after the Governor's proclamation, October 13, Co. A, First Regiment, OMV, under Capt. A.V. Wilson, started upriver from Portland.[34] Three weeks later in excess of 850 men were poised on the fringe of Indian Country at The Dalles.[35] The feat of dispatching armies into northern and southern Oregon in the face of prevailing panic, basic unpreparedness, problematical communications and political rivalry, was a striking accomplishment.

The men poured into Portland from Oregon's nine northern counties except Co. B, Wasco County, mustered into service at The Dalles. Every company exceeded the 60 rank and file specified in the proclamation with the exception of Marion County's Co. K, made up of 30 tough, experienced French Canadian guides and scouts. Curry expressed special gratitude upon learning of Narcisse Cornoyer's organization of a company "we need . . . very much."[36] No county lagged seriously and each company proceeded to Portland with dispatch where they mustered into service before leaving for The Dalles.

Some units marched over the Barlow Road that skirted Mt. Hood's southern slope. More troops were moved by boat or on barges towed down the Willamette and up the Columbia to the Lower Cascades. Here they disembarked, marched to the Upper Cascades to reboard the steamboat for the last stretch to The Dalles. High winds, thick fog or varied equipment could occasion changes in the route to include a crossing to the Oregon shore at Dog (Hood) River, thence on land to The Dalles. Sometimes a crossing was made at the mouth of Sandy River, then along the Washington bank to the Cascades, and a recrossing at Wind River, with the remaining distance to The Dalles being on land. This tedious process stemmed directly from the long segments of Columbia shoreline that were not suitable for trails or roads.[37]

Colonel James Nesmith, from the first days of the war, recognized the exasperating difficulty of moving freight over this complicated course.[38] He foresaw the grave consequences of the unavoidable unloading and reloading of man, beast and supplies at the Cascades. He was deeply and correctly concerned "that there will be some delay in forwarding our supplies from this point." Curry promptly assigned

26

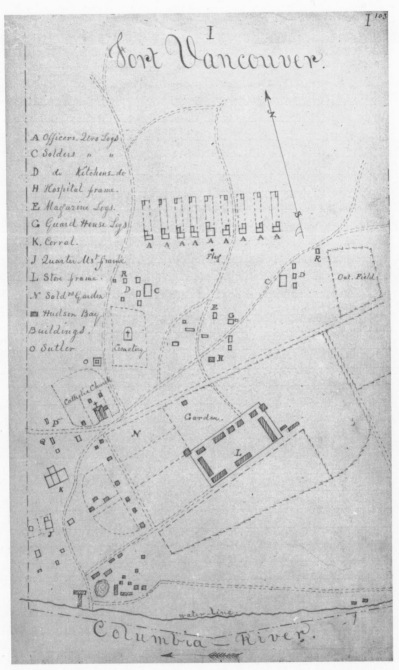

Fort Vancouver.

Cyrus Olney as permanent freight expediter at this key junction. Probably nothing more was humanly possible in the presence of an insurmountable combination of nature's forces. Nesmith's most pessimistic fears were fully vindicated in the first week of the war despite the expediter's diligent attention.[39]

Whatever the foreseen hazards of employing water transportation for freight, Nesmith emphatically preferred that the troops move by boat. "The Dalles can be reached much sooner by this than the Cascade [mountain] route," he informed Curry. Some companies did march to The Dalles over the Barlow Road, but most went by water in compliance with Nesmith's directive. The obstacle-strewn route to the border of enemy country accurately presaged the frustrating sufferings of subsequent months.

The first Volunteers to leave Portland boarded the *Fashion* for Vancouver at six o'clock on the evening of Oct. 15, 1855. They were mustered into service earlier that Saturday, a short two days after the governor's initial call. Their first stop was at Fort Vancouver, where they expected to obtain necessary equipment that Curry had requisitioned from the U.S. Army Commissary and Quartermaster of that post. Hopes were dashed by Lt. John Withers' refusal to issue anything until the men were mustered into the service of the United States. Curry acceded to this demand only to withdraw his assent, lest he lose control of the Volunteers. The impasse was resolved, after nearly a full day's delay, by Lt. Theodore Eckerson assuming the full risk for honoring Curry's request.[40]

Patriotic speeches and the presentation of the colors consumed part of an idle Sunday and cleared the way for a Monday morning departure from Vancouver. After disembarking, they camped at the Lower Cascades that first night. Tuesday, October 16, they sloshed their way to the Upper Cascades where they were drenched for two nights and a day while waiting for the *Mary* to carry them to The Dalles, Thursday, Oct. 18, 1855.[41]

They spent a full day in this brawling frontier settlement before setting off for "Three Mile creek above The Dalles where we made our permanent encampment while we shall remain here." There was slim likelihood of anyone leaving before horses, tents, blankets, ammunition and food were issued.[42]

Other volunteer companies joined Co. A as quickly as wind, fog, rain, hopelessly inadequate transport, poor horses and short supplies permitted. Co. C, Clackamas County, and Co. D, Washington County came by way of the Barlow Road. Co. E, Yamhill County, and Co. F, Marion County, moved by boat but only after fog forced Co. E to

28

Upstream approach to The Cascades.

remain aboard the *Gazelle, Fashion,* and *Multnomah*[43] until needed visibility came with daylight. High winds and rough water forced Co. F to leave the boats at Cape Horn and go by land to the Upper Cascades. Co. D arrived at The Dalles October 25; Cos. C and E came in the following day; Cos. F and H, Linn County, encamped November 1; and Co. I, Benton County, arrived on November 3.[44]

While movement of men went forward expeditiously, the transportation of freight was quite another matter. The direst anxieties over the snarled Cascades were abundantly fulfilled, while all of the Volunteers, except Co. A, were still enroute to The Dalles. Nesmith's forebodings anticipated the fate of future major shipments since "Even the small supply of ammunition &c purchased . . ., on the 17th inst., at Vancouver, which came to The Cascades with us, has not reached this point." He noted further that "If this delay is to be continued, that point might as well be, for all practical purposes, in the hands of the enemy, and will prevent the command from taking the field this winter.[45] These black presentiments were justified before the Volunteers ever left The Dalles. While still encamped it was

29

reported that, "the volunteers are sadly disappointed in not getting supplies from the Willamette Valley. *For God's sake send them supplies.*" No one complained of hunger yet but "we must have more supplies, we must have horses; we must have arms, ammunition, &c."[46]

None of this succeeded in staying Curry's order for Nesmith to proceed "into the Yakima country" with Cos. C, D, E, F and G. (Co. A came later as escort to a pack train.) They got off to a ragged start, November 1, with parts of Cos. C and E delayed in crossing the Columbia because "the wind blowing a perfect hurricane, prevents the steamer *Wasco* from getting across the river." Co. E was held up because "all of their supplies had not reached them." The officers' conviction that it was "almost impossible . . . to get supplies for only ten days" were not shared by Curry. He adopted the Quartermaster and Commissary Departments' position, "that your supply is sufficient, with prudent management, for thirty days." This veiled rebuke was penned when not a pound of coffee was on hand and while Curry was personally present at The Dalles. Someone was in error![47]

In any event, 485 Volunteers set out to overtake the Regulars, Nov. 3, 1855, and camped within four miles of Major Rains by the next evening. The military successes of the cooperating forces up to November 7 were restricted to capturing a cow, a calf and 80 horses.[48] Capt. Thomas Cornelius with 69 Volunteers, while searching intensively for Indians and stray cattle on November 8, had two men severely wounded in a three-hour fight against 100 warriors.

The Regulars and remaining Volunteers, on that day, marched directly to the Yakima River instead of paralleling Cornelius' crescent-shaped path. Late in the afternoon the U.S. troops reached the south bank of the river where they exchanged harmless shots with Indians on the opposite shore of the deep, swift water. Sixty Volunteers from Cos. C and F bolted forward from their camp, forded the stream with Sheridan's Dragoons, and drove the enemy up the hill.[49]

A similar indecisive encounter began after breakfast, November 9, with a sweep through the brush that sent Indians scurrying to prepared positions atop the two buttes between which the river flowed (now Union Gap). A few rounds from the howitzer failed to dislodge the taunting natives from the effective protection afforded by the steep buttes. A promiscuous charge by Regulars and Volunteers, maddened by the jeers, chased off the abusive defenders. A victory bonfire was lighted with reckless exultation before the whites retired and some 300 Indians reoccupied the heights.[50]

*S.S. Multnomah.*

A touch of real military conduct was in the organized assault of the following morning that routed the defenders, killed two of them, but failed utterly to cut off the escape of the rest. Hours of futile hunting made clear the clean getaway of people and stock. The sting of this successful flight was not blunted by the stray cattle and horses herded into the camp on Ahtanum Creek.[51]

It was thought that the Indians had fled toward the Columbia River. Nesmith, nevertheless, left for Naches Pass November 11, with 250 volunteers and the Dragoons, to oppose a surprise attack from that direction should one develop. They planned to trap any Indians hiding in the west between themselves and a relief detachment presumably enroute from Fort Steilacoom. A three-day snowfall and the absence of any Indian or white signs turned Nesmith back to the camp twelve miles west of Two Buttes, and two miles down Ahtanum Creek from unoccupied St. Joseph's Catholic Mission.[52]

While Nesmith was looking for Capt. Maurice Maloney's detachment (which had turned back on October 29), idle Volunteers and Regulars looted the mission and rifled caches around the property. Men paraded derisively in vestments taken from the church; Regulars burglarized the buildings: vegetables, flour, sacramental wine, a half keg of powder, and whatever was moveable were stolen, divided up,

31

The Restored St. Joseph's Mission, Ahtanum.

or destroyed. The mission was reduced to ashes by a deliberately set fire that climaxed the frolic, Nov. 14, 1855. They were more convincing as common pillagers than Indian fighters.[53]

The morning after this destructive romp, they took up the line of march, covered ten miles, and encamped in the Simcoe Valley where a council of officers agreed upon a direct return to The Dalles. Two weeks in snow without sufficient rations, blankets, tents, clothes or forage had greatly weakened men and animals. Any projected campaigning in the Walla Walla region was unthinkable under prevailing conditions.[54]

All of the force reached the scene of Haller's defeat in time for a guided tour by the vanquished commander, November 16. Nesmith, at least, was convinced by what he heard and saw that the ill-fated column was overwhelmed by a superior force on October 7. The remains of two killed on that day were found scattered on the ground. Their skulls, spinal column and a few bones were reinterred with Rains reading the military burial service during which "the escort fired 3 vollies over their graves." It was a grimly chilling reminder, to twice thwarted avengers, of the Yakima's victory.[55]

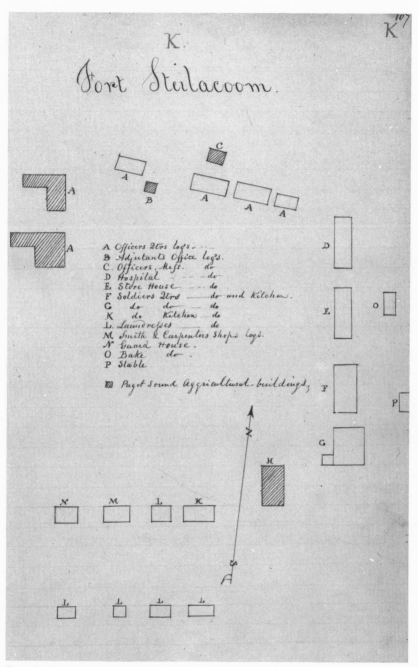

K.

Fort Steilacoom.

A  Officers Qtrs logs.
B  Adjutants Office logs.
C  Officers Mess.      do
D  Hospital          do
E  Store House       do
F  Soldiers Qtrs     do and Kitchen.
G  do    do    do
K  do    Kitchen  do
L  Laundresses      do
M  Smith & Carpenters Shops logs.
N  Guard House.
O  Bake    do.
P  Stable

▨  Puget Sound Aggricultural buildings;

Fort Steilacoom.

33

None of this was seen by Co. A; it was still hopeful of meeting the main command. They had left The Dalles November 7 with 45 pack animals carrying ten days' provisions for Nesmith's right column. The usual route to Five Mile Camp, thence over the mountains, took them to the Klickitat River by November 10. Heavy snow the next day buried the trail and caused them to lose their bearings. Instead of wandering about, they prudently waited for Capt. Narcisse Cornoyer's experienced Co. K to rescue them, November 14. The two companies marched together, survived "a terrible snow storm," and overtook the main body in the snow-encrusted Simcoe Mountains November 17.[56]

One dispatch they delivered was Curry's order to proceed to the Walla Walla country. Each company captain, in a written report, reaffirmed the lack of healthy men and animals for continued operations in the field. Co. E had a "few" men and horses fit for service; 65 horses but no men in Co. F were fit; and Cos. C, D and G registered a resounding "none" in both categories. A council of officers concurred in the utter impracticability of complying with the order and continued on to The Dalles in conformity with their previous decision.[57]

Most of the command was left near good grass at the Klickitat River, while Nesmith hastened ahead into The Dalles, 25 miles away, where he arrived November 19. He insisted that Curry grasp the fact that further winter campaigning with enfeebled men and horses was impossible. The obstacles of transport and supply, to him, were so obviously colossal that he probably anticipated a speedy order disbanding the volunteer units still in the field.[58]

Curry's failure to take executive action was responsible for Nesmith

discharging about one hundred and twenty-five men from my regiment ... A large number of the men were averse to going to Walla Walla, from the fact of being mounted on horses totally unfit to make the trip. As there are no horses here suitable to remount the men, I resolved to grant their applications to be discharged, deeming it worse than useless to retain a large unmounted force at this place to consume our scanty supplies.[59]

His entreaties for basic supplies and equipment dated from the very recruitment of the Volunteers. Repeated representations were muted, apparently, by the more dexterous personnel in the Quartermaster and Commissary departments who adduced figures to prove the complete adequacy of subsistence supplies. Nesmith and his men had only experienced the chronic insufficiency of resources in the

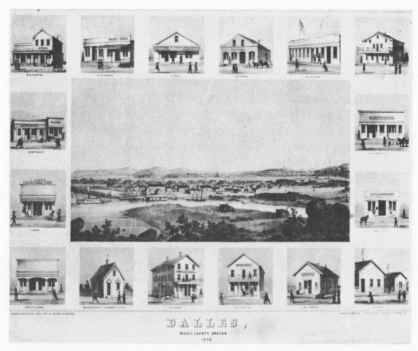

*Dalles, Oregon, 1858.*

field and had never been able to "eat" the figures proving the existence of sufficient food. He had determined, presumably, to separate himself from a situation in which a bookkeeper's page was preferred to the word of an unfed soldier.[60]

The Colonel arrived in Portland December 1, and on December 4 resigned from the Volunteers "because of serious sickness in his family." True, his wife and daughter were ill at the moment, but his action was known to spring from the demonstrated futility of continuing pursuit under countless adverse conditions.[61]

The total failure to corner the Yakimas and the abrupt resignation of the commanding colonel had no visible effect on Curry's determination to send a search mission along the Walla Walla River. Lt. Col. James Kelly received orders Nov. 3, 1855, to prepare the left column, First Regiment, OMV, "to be in readiness for instant service." A few days later Curry appointed Maj. Mark Chinn as battalion commander, and left Kelly in command at The Dalles, lest the latter be absent from the opening sessions of the Oregon Legislative Coun-

35

cil, of which he was a member. Circumstances would overrule these well-intentioned dispositions.[62]

On the day when Nesmith was looking for Indians, Maloney was in the deep snows toward Naches Pass, and Co. A's men stumbling about in a Klickitat snowstorm, November 11, Chinn was bewailing the disheartening hindrances delaying his departure for the Walla Walla. Very high prices were demanded for many items he sought and he was forced to procure cattle by compulsion. This odious situation was blamed on "the discouragement thrown in our way by some of the U.S. officers." Their

> talks of illegality and of the delays of Congress are made to our prejudice; the citizens grow alarmed and refuse to sell but at exorbitant prices, and this again is used to prevent any sales, for suspicions are sown abroad that these purchases will, if ever paid, be greatly cut down. Thus we are stopped.

Bitterness and disillusionment are evident in the disclosure that

> The Hudson's Bay Company, a foreign corporation, has done us much service, and acted with the greatest humanity. We feel sometimes that these are our fellow-citizens, and that representatives of the United States government are foreigners, and not even friendly allies.[63]

Chinn started for Walla Walla the next day, Nov. 12, 1855, with Co. B, First Regiment, mostly made up of men from Wasco County. They overtook Co. H, Linn County, at the mouth of the Deschutes River. The combined force encamped at Wells Springs, November 17. Here their plans and those of many others were radically altered by an urgent appeal for help from Narcisse Raymond in the name of the white and halfbreed settlers in the Walla Walla Valley. John McBean and Augustin DeLore, the expressmen, had similar letters for Governor Curry and Nathan Olney, sub-agent at The Dalles.[64] They brought the dismaying news that Peu-Peu-Mox-Mox, the Walla Walla chief, had plundered Fort Walla Walla, razed Brooke, Bomford and Noble's property, threatened the settlers and had a thousand warriors blocking the road to Walla Walla. James Sinclair assured Chinn "that the position of [the Indians was] unassailable" with the number of Volunteers in his command.

Chinn needed no more prompting to order the construction of a fortification on the Umatilla River. They built a 100-foot-square stockade, with two bastions of round logs, and a stock corral outside the palisade. Here he would encamp until "either reinforcements arrive or the right column may create a diversion in my favor."

36

Nesmith's right column didn't create a diversion for anyone but it did arrive at The Dalles soon after Chinn's appeal for assistance.

Additional troops pushed forward to the cottonwood stockade, Fort Henrietta (named in honor of Major Haller's wife), as swiftly as tired men could move. Cos. I and A left The Dalles November 22, with Plympton Kelly recording the event as the opening entry in his diary. Co. K came two days later, and Co. F marched on November 26. Co. C was assigned as escort to provision trains and guard of the Deschutes River ferry, and Cos. D and E were scouting for Indians and cattle until summoned two weeks later to bolster the embattled Volunteers at Walla Walla.[65]

The six companies, A, B, F, H, I and K, some 339 men under James Kelly's command, left Fort Henrietta for Walla Walla at sunset, December 2. The snow, rain and 18 hours without unsaddling the horses evoked Plympton Kelly's plaint that "I have not often endured more suffering than I have on this march." He could not know that this doleful refrain would characterize as yet unwritten entries in his diary. His would be the best personal record of subsequent events to survive the war.[66]

Very little of importance escaped his notice or a mention in the daily entries. The 30-mile ride through the night from Fort Henrietta ended on the Walla Walla River at 10 a.m., December 3. The Volunteers encamped, breakfasted, and some still found energy enough to visit the ruins of Fort Walla Walla. The next morning those eager for a fight scrambled in reply to a report that 25 Indians were crossing the Columbia. One Indian was thought killed in the ensuing long-range exchange of shots across the river.

A realistic recognition of the enfeebled condition of almost half the horses resulted in some 150 men, including Plympton Kelly, being assigned to move the command's baggage to the mouth of the Touchet River where they would guard it. Half of these men, under Major Chinn, would see combat soon because of the sudden developments confronting Kelly and his 200 men mounted on the stronger horses.

These troops were probing up the Touchet in search of the enemy on December 5 when, without warning, Peu-Peu-Mox-Mox and 40 of his men approached Major Cornoyer under a white flag. The chief was taken promptly to Kelly. The Indians wanted, according to the chief, to settle all differences without fighting and to make full payment for all property destroyed or stolen. Kelly retorted coldly that the Volunteers were ready to fight and if Peu-Peu-Mox-Mox "did not surrender himself and arms" he could leave under his white flag with the expectation of a battle. They surrendered as prisoners of war

Governor and Mrs. George L. Curry.                    Oregon Historical Society

and were put under guard. The baggage detachment was ordered to send a 75-man reinforcement because Kelly apparently intended to goad the Indians into a major attack by the severity of his conditions for peace.

The Volunteers continued up the Touchet throughout Thursday, December 6. The release of two prisoners as emissaries failed to entice any of the hovering Indians. Kelly's demand that all arms, ammunition and stock be surrendered was equally fruitless. After preventing one escape that night all prisoners were tied securely.

Whatever were the subtle intentions of Peu-Peu-Mox-Mox's voluntary appearance or of Kelly's nettling demands, they became unimportant as the long weekend of December 7 unfolded. Early on that Friday morning, Indians on the surrounding hills demanded the release of their chief and threatened war against any further advance into the Walla Walla Valley.[67] The command broke camp and had moved less than a mile when some Indians opened fire upon two herdsmen. The Volunteers' instant charge turned into a 10 mile fighting chase until their "horses began to fail and the Indians began

38

to increase in number." Two miles below Whitman's Mission, near La Rocque's cabin, was the scene of the severest struggle. The savage four-day battle saw

the hostiles creeping upon us in the shelter of hollows or skulking or lying flat behind clumps of sage brush, while much of the time we could use our horses to no advantage, but had to fight on the ground and behind bushes, the same as the Indians.

After several hours of firing on December 10, Co. A lunged forward and put the fleeing Indians into headlong rout. The opportune arrival that evening of Cos. D and E, with a fresh supply of ammunition, was the final discouragement to any renewal of combat.[68]

Ferocity marked these four days. Indians killed, scalped, and tauntingly dangled the bloody trophy in front of former comrades. The Volunteers cut down Peu-Peu-Mox-Mox and four of his companions in an alleged escape on the night of December 7. Plympton Kelly contended that they were killed because "they refused to be tied." A whole week later the diary unmistakably records that "yesterday [December 13] Peu-Peu-Mox-Mox was taken up by Dr. Shaw and his ears cut of[f] and to day he has ben taken out and subject to further indignities." A measure of the ghoulish loathing is revealed in a non-participating observer's comment that the dead chief's

whole scalp was taken from his head and cut up into 20 pieces, his skull divided equally, for Buttons-his ears preserved in a bottle of spirits-and large strips of his skin cut off *along his back to be made into Razor stroups* — such is Indian warfare . . .

Besides these nauseous ventings of terrifying rancor, there were an estimated 75 dead Indians, although only 39 bodies were counted. The tally of wounded natives was unknown. Six Volunteers died in or after the engagement, and 15 were wounded in this solitary major battle of the entire campaign.[70]

Not an Indian could be seen on Tuesday morning, December 11. A two-day search made it reasonably certain that some went north and others simply faded into the countryside. This left nothing for the foeless Volunteers except to establish winter quarters.

Camp Curry was set up about two miles above the Whitman Mission site on December 15. The dragging months spent here were marked by maddening cold, tedium and hunger. They were tortured before the recent battle by numbing winter. Now, scarcely settled in their new camp, heavy snow and piercing twenty below zero weather afflicted them. Any exposed bodily surface was frostbitten, but especially did the wounded suffer. Lack of food and exposure, not surprisingly, killed some horses.[71]

Jamming ice stopped all boat traffic on the Columbia, further delaying badly needed rations. Officers and men, officially and in private, deplored their gnawing want. A full two weeks earlier, November 26, Nesmith had sought the Governor's help because The Dalles "commissary department is almost destitute of every indispensable article of subsistence, and particularly flour and fresh beef." He added, almost curtly, that "unless this deficiency was corrected immediately by forwarding the necessary subsistence the troops would have to be recalled."[72] Subsequent failure to heed his admonition did not disprove the validity of his analysis.

Cornelius confirmed the obvious with his admission that the Volunteers had not pursued the Indians "in consequence of hour horses being werked and having no supplys." Their straitened condition was clear in another letter to the Governor that told plainly

> ... of the great want of subsistence for the troops in the commissary department [at The Dalles]; of the beggarly absence of the means for transportation at the command of the regimental quarter-master; and the extreme embarrassments to which we have thus far been subjected in procuring supplies, stores, ammunition, &c from the Willamette Valley.[73]

This report, as others in like vein, stirred no ripple on the pond of official imperviousness. Curry's refusal to acknowledge what was known by every man in the field borders upon fantasy. He accepted official reassurance of the complete adequacy of rations, while some Volunteers were so hungry as to slaughter 12 cattle belonging to the Indians and "left them laying on the hides. It turned cold that night the thermometer going down to 22 below zero, and we stayed there until we ate them up, chipping the meat off with axes."[74] Again and again, Plympton Kelly's diary returns to the shortage of food, the search for beef cattle, and a constant alert for food caches. The weather-induced irregularity of pack trains aggravated an already trying situation.

Idleness, cold, hunger and deeply rooted enmities all contributed to the unsavory reputation acquired by the Volunteers in the course of the winter. Friendly Indians and French Canadian farmers in the Walla Walla Valley were victimized most often. Narcisse Raymond and his Walla Walla neighbors appealed to the Volunteers for protection when they returned to Henry Chase's Touchet claim from their wartime haven with the Nez Perce tribe. Co. K responded to the request by escorting the settlers and some 100 friendly Indians to their permanent camp on Mill Creek, about 10 miles from the former Whitman Mission.[75] Despite the shielding presence of Cornoyer's company, within 10 days Raymond was writing ruefully:

We were very glad to here [hear] that the Volunteers had whipped the Indians, which saved our lives, but sorry to find that they had stolen our caches and robbed us of all our provisions, killing our stock, &c, and the officers had no control over them.

A month of nervous living is mirrored in a later complaint that

If we were in danger when among the Indians, we are no better now, they [Volunteers] are determined to starve us & take our lives. They come everyday & take our stock at our doors & when we remonstrate, threaten to shoot us . . .

Other victims of the restless marauders used sharper words describing their thieving vandalism. John F. Noble reported disgustedly that "Lt. Harding of Co. A, with some d---d infernal rascals broke open" George Bomford's trunks (cached on the Brooke, Bomford and Noble Waiilatpu farm) "and took out everything, read his private letters and scattered them all along the road, also his sketches, and are now wearing his clothes; threw away his sisters daguerreotype, which Mr. Jeffries has kindly picked up and brought to me."[76] Plympton Kelly "got a volume of Dannas minerology" from one of the trunks.[77]

A few days later Major Chinn tried to curb some of the excesses by warning the entire command that French settlers' and friendly Indians' persons and property were to be respected and "that no more caches should be raised but by the men in the service of the commissary 3) that no more hogs be killed 4) that there be no more stealing."[78]

Defiance showed itself the very next evening with a report "that Nathan Olney and others wer driving of[f] a large number of horses." Governor Curry was "informed that about 250 head of stock have been seized in the Indian country by irresponsible men and driven into the vicinity of The Dalles." Some observers voiced alarm that unless the Volunteers were arrested "in their brigand actions," the friendly Indians "will save themselves by flying to the homes of their relations the Nez Perces, who have promised them help, and then all the Indians of Oregon would join in the common defence until they be entirely exterminated."[79]

These genuinely harmful spoliations of friends were part of a dreary picture made up of hostile weather, sporadic raids, occasional scouting duty, never plentiful food, and a burning desire to escape the monotony. These factors bore no resemblance to the originally planned decisive winter campaign. Frozen weeks, used up horses, scanty supplies in all categories, and a wraith-like enemy conspired against any serious pursuit before the early part of March.

41

When Cornelius replaced Nesmith as regimental colonel, Dec. 19, 1855, he expected "to prosecute the war with all possible vigger." A week later he was "waiting for orders from the governor to no [know] whether we will be discharged or not." He was disappointed, if he was truly expecting a release.

Pressing problems, instead, ripened in clusters. While worries about supplies, spies and effective troops weighed upon him, his very right to command was challenged by Major Chinn. The absence of a formal colonel's commission confirming his election to that office, was probably less significant than the personal pique Chinn felt over not being elected to replace Nesmith. The Governor suspended Chinn for insubordination, only to restore him to duty ten days later, Jan. 23, 1856, amidst circulated rumors of strong political pressure. Plympton Kelly records the arrival of the tardy commission and the departure of the alleged culprit.[81]

Cornelius exercised restraint in ordering Chinn during the sticky episode, without shrinking from the depressing need of feeding the men and preparing for a spring offensive. Four hundred recruits responded to the governor's appeal for troops to replace the resigned and discharged Volunteers. This influx raised the enlisted rank and file of the First Regiment, OMV, to an all-time high of 901.

The comforting presence of augmented strength was sternly tempered by unimproved transport facilities. The third week in January the command was "out of flour sugar and coffee salt and tobacco but we had a pack train come in today with about four thousand pounds of flour."[82]

Even more worrisome was an evident lack of ardor among some for any ill-provisioned drive against the Indians. These differences were aired with non-military candor by the reluctant citizen soldiers. Company A's own A. V. Wilson maintained tenaciously that the previous November's debacle furnished conclusive proof of "the fallacy of attempting a winter campaign against the Yakima Indians." He warned Cornelius in an apparent attempt to cool his zeal for a new march with insufficient resources that

> ... To go without twenty days rations and a good supply of proper ammunition and a force of four hundred men would be madness in the extreme. You have a more formidable enemy to contend against than you have any idea of. And to fail in an expedition would be ruinous in the extreme and you must remember that this is not a Cayuse war, and that a mere opinion must not hazzard the success of the troops but that the utmost prudence and discretion must be exercised to insure its *certain* success.

42

Should the colonel's memory have grown dim, Wilson reminded him without apology that "I was instrumental in placing you in the position you now occupy and you may imagine the solicitude I have to see you conduct the campaign with honor to yourself and credit to the regiment." Wilson's unclouded recollection of vainly stumbling after the Yakimas in blinding snows dampened his eagerness for restaging the spectacle in less familiar country. Nor did he hide from the fact that "the volunteers are almost entirely destitute of supplies, clothing, boots, and shoes, blankets and other necessaries absolutely requisite to advance and cross Snake river."[83]

Two sizable requisitions submitted by Cornelius, Feb. 1, 1856, document his awareness of the gross and glaring deficiencies. From the Commissary he asked 17 tons of flour, 3,600 pounds of sugar, a half ton of soap and 300 pounds of rice among many other items. The request to the quartermaster listed 200 pair of boots, 300 pair of shoes, 100,000 percussion caps and 20 good rifles.[84]

The endless struggle for daily rations immeasurably complicated the separate project of amassing supplies for a new campaign. The command, at all times, was so taken up with survival that each pack train's progress was of vital interest. The five wagons delayed by melting snow at Ten Mile Creek and Tom Hubbard's arrival there with 15 following wagons were reported to Cornelius without delay. This particular train was ordered to unload a ton and a half of flour at Fort Henrietta, before hastening on to the Walla Walla Valley. These wagons, thought to be carrying food for troops almost ready to move, were found to be "burdened with a six months' supply of tobacco and coffee far beyond our requirements."[85]

Cornelius labored to correct other haunting shortages. He hoped to replace jaded or lost horses by sending Lts. Myers and W. H. Wright "to negotiate for the purchase of 300 head of good serviceable riding horses" from the Nez Perce Indians. Ten days later, March 6, they were back with 42 horses that the quartermaster purchased without hesitation.[86]

Other needs clamored for attention before there could be any success. Reports placed the hostiles, families, stock and personal effects on the far side of the Snake River. This contingency was in mind, Feb. 4, 1856, when Cornelius ordered the quartermaster "to build six boats of a size and strength sufficient to enable me to cross my command over Snake or Columbia rivers . . ." Five weeks later whipsawed boards, pine knot tar and scavenged nails had been fashioned into the required craft.[87]

Each semi-overcome hindrance was supplanted, it seemed, by one

43

a little worse. A pack train of tobacco and coffee for hungry men might make sense to a bureaucrat; but the loss of pack mules themselves to the enemy could be appreciated by any reasonable person. Midway in February, Plympton Kelly headed an eight-man escort for B. F. Dowell's train on a round trip from Camp Cornelius to Fort Henrietta. Nothing marred the journey until about midnight Sunday, February 24, when camped on Wild Horse Creek Kelly was "waked by the yelling of the Indians" who were driving off the horses and mules. No supplies were taken, but the stampeding of some 30 pack animals brought further stress on already strained communications.

Plympton's first concern was guarding the supplies until removed from their vulnerable position. He sent two men to headquarters for wagons, while he dug in at camp and asked Co. B (engaged in cattle hunting) to stay close until the pack loads were safe. Although 25 men were sent in search of the stolen animals, over two weeks passed before Capt. A. Rivais, Co. K, received an order to return to their owner "all mules in your command that belonged to Dowells pack train and which have been recaptured from the Indians by you."[88]

The diary gives no hint of any reprimand for losing the mules and horses. Cornelius did blame the loss on the escort's failure to exercise proper care. The Governor, replying to Cornelius, "very much regretted" what had happened and pointedly insisted that, "A commissioned officer should have been in charge, however, and I have to request you again to place all details for escort duty under command of commissioned officers."[89]

This latest order from Curry must have bemused a headquarters staff whose command had lost a large number of horses on February 27, only two days after Plympton's train was struck. Nor is there any word of Curry's advice when told that Colonel Kelly lost all but one horse from his camp on the Umatilla during the same period.[90]

Whether each reverse stiffened Cornelius' resolve to push ahead or simply spurred his efforts before something worse befell the enterprise cannot be determined. His fixed purpose is unmistakable, however perplexing his motivation. Three days before leaving camp he dispatched Lt. W. Stillwell with 25 men to meet Sam Johnson's wagon train loaded with much wanted ammunition. The precious lead and powder were to be speeded directly to headquarters in the lightest wagon.

Should this train be carrying no ammunition, "200 lbs. lead, 15,000 percussion caps, 200 lbs. fine canister powder" were to be obtained at The Dalles. The order was to be executed "within the shortest possible space of time, and strictly to the letter." One can concur heartily

44

with Plympton's trenchant observation that it was "a pretty time indeed to be sending for ammunition."[91]

A flury of orders filled the last days before the men "would cross Snake river and give Camiakin a fight . . . and clean Mr. Indians out." Commanding officers were instructed, March 5, 1856, "to make an inspection of arms and ammunition in their respective commands." The following day came the fateful order to "issue but one half (½) rations of flour to the troops on this (East) side of the Umatilla river." This spartan measure, necessitated by dismal weeks of erratic food deliveries, deepened the disaffection in two companies of recruits. None of this would lighten Cornelius' burden, once they were in the field.[92]

Company commanders were alerted, March 7, to break camp two days later, Sunday, March 9. Fifty men under Lt. Charles Pillow (including Plympton Kelly) were to establish a supply encampment near Fort Walla Walla. They were enjoined to scout the area, watch for canoes on the Columbia and Walla Walla rivers, and "maintain a vigilant guard and exercise every precaution against surprise." The detachment's separation from the main command explains why Plympton's diary contains only reported news of the campaign until April 5, 1856, when he rejoined the main body of troops during its final march to The Dalles.[93]

Despite inadequate food, arms, horses, stores and reserves for the undertaking, they marched on that bleak Sunday morning. Only the day before, Cornelius penned the plaintive hope

> that officers and soldiers will be obedient to orders, preserve a kindly disposition toward each other and equally strive to win a noble triumph over our common enemy thus silencing forever the faults [false] statements of those persons who are interested to defame the reputation of the Oregon volunteers.[94]

Some of the nearly 500 men fulfilled his hopes; and others far exceeded his worst apprehensions.

Their search for the foe took them down the Touchet Valley to the Snake where they turned up the Columbia for 10 miles. Still hunting for Indians, they next skirted along the Snake as far as the Palouse River up which they probed for 8 miles and encamped, March 17, 1856. There they stayed until the 23rd, while hunger-rooted mutiny shredded the command.[95]

An urgent plea for rations was rushed to Walla Walla too late to prevent the violent eruption of smoldering resentment on March 20. Three days of horse meat diet enkindled the outburst. Many men, especially from Cos. A and D, Recruiting Battalion, were set on going

45

to The Dalles without leave. Cornelius ordered the companies to parade under arms at nine on that Thursday morning. The air was taut as the veteran companies "were formed, guns in hand, facing the sullen mutineers" across a hollow square. Major Curl encouraged the mutineers with his declaration that "he would march his command back forthwith" because the Governor had no intention of their moving until properly provisioned.

Cornelius, Kelly, Cornoyer and Pvt. George Shiel, each in turn stressed the need for sound judgment and abominated any kind of desertion. Shiel was effectively persuasive[96] and Kelly defused the crisis by boldly asking

> if they had enlisted for a May day picnic or merely for sport. He informed them he would bleach their bones on the prairie if they attempted to return. He then ordered them to dismount, which they did. Obedience to this order saved many lives and the reputation of the regiment.

The arrival of rations two days later steadied the situation and got the troops in motion again.[97]

They covered 65 arduous miles, March 23-26, through the harsh country lying between the Upper Palouse and 10 or 12 miles below Priest's Rapids on the Columbia. After a day's rest, they continued for 40 miles downstream to a camp opposite the mouth of the Yakima River.

The combined expedition ended here with the division of the command into several groups each with a specific assignment. Major Curl with veteran Cos. H and K, together with the recently rebellious Cos. A and D of recruits, were to scout and hold the Walla Walla country as far as the Blue Mountains. Captain Cason and Co. E were to approach The Dalles by way of Wild Horse Creek, Umatilla River, John Day River, Eureka Valley and Warm Springs. Co. B under Capt. John T. Jeffries, would level Fort Henrietta on the way home to Wasco County. Pillow and his men at Fort Walla Walla were to dispose of all stores and rejoin Co. A on its concluding prowl up the Yakima River. Not even all of these "final" dispositions were permanent.[98]

Lt. Richard Caldwell, Co. D, hastened to Fort Walla Walla to arrange the shipment of 15 days' subsistence for 500 men to the mouth of the Yakima River. While returning from his mission, he unluckily met Major Curl who took 400 lbs. of flour from the 1,000 pounds being transported. Caldwell's remonstrances were spurned but not Cornelius' curt instruction to the insubordinate officer: "Lieut. Col. James K. Kelley having been ordered to the command of the forces on the

*Upper Cascades, Columbia River, 1867.*

south side of the Columbia you will immediately report to him for duty." It was finally brutally clear that repeated lawlessness, even though hunger-inspired, was intolerable.[99]

The imminent campaign by Col. George Wright's U.S. Ninth Infantry was furnishing a convenient occasion for disbanding most of the weary and unruly Volunteers. The U.S. forces would presumably harry the Indians, pacify the land, and protect the settlers as the Volunteers fancied themselves doing during the long, raw winter. Wright's advance was cut short, however, before it was a day old, by the uncowed natives.

Wright had overcome most of the familiar hindrances hounding his weeks of prudent preparation. Superior Army resources help explain his slightly better performance in surmounting barriers. Transportation jumbles, especially the unchanged muddle at the Cascades, detained him. The inevitable accumulation of freight at this key point made its uninterrupted retention supremely important. The detachment posted here was adequate until transferred to Fort Steilacoom by Gen. John E. Wool, Wright's superior officer. This change left only 8 men to guard this vital site on the day Wright left Fort Dalles, March

47

26, 1856.[100] The 500 man command encamped on Five Mile Creek that night. Word of the bloody attack on the Cascades overtook them here.

They moved back to The Dalles on the double at daybreak, March 27, whence the steamers *Mary* and *Wasco* speeded 300 of them to the embattled area by dawn of the 28. They joined with Lt. Phil Sheridan's force from Fort Vancouver in driving off the besiegers. Forty swiftly recruited Portland civilians as well as Capt. H. D. Wallen's 37 U.S. troopers were too late to help.[101]

The far-ranging effects of this single raid must have exceeded the wildest expectations of the Indians. The assault, defense, recapture and subsequent punitive measures resulted in 20 Indian and 15 white deaths, along with 22 known white wounded. Wright cancelled outright his projected sortie against the Walla Wallas and committed his entire strength to a dogged, fruitless movement through the Yakima lands. Return of the Volunteers to their homes was slowed and there was even raised some serious question about their immediate discharge.

The almost universal panic among the settlers was the most striking aftermath of the attack. Facts inflated by rumor induced a stampede. People fled from their farms to Fort Vancouver, while some army men encouraged their own wives to flee to the sheltering stockade of the nearby Hudson's Bay Company. Still other dependents were packed off to Portland or to San Francisco for a visit. Not a few families, many weeks before this solitary attack, had closed their businesses and departed permanently.[102]

None of this affected the starved, bone-weary Volunteers intent upon reaching The Dalles by way of the Yakima country. Two hundred and forty-one emaciated men crossed the Columbia, March 31, 1856, and remained at Camp Yakima until April 4. Thence they moved to a spot opposite Fort Walla Walla whither all usable provisions were ferried before Pillow's detachment rejoined Co. A, April 5.

Next day's tramp was 30 rainy miles over rocky, sandy, sage and grass-covered ground to a camp on the Yakima River. Here the proposed Oregon constitutional convention was voted on and defeated by Co. A as it was by the majority of Oregonians. Voting so delayed Monday's start that only 10 miles were made before encamping. Twenty miles on Tuesday and 14 on Wednesday, April 9, brought them near the mouth of Canyon (Cold) Creek by nightfall.[103]

Thursday's tragedy is captured in the diary's attack record that

early this morning Captain Wilson Hembree and Wilber with 6 other men started out to reconnoiter crossing over to the right of the creek and when they had got near the sumit of the hills the Indians

48

charged on them from 3 sides Captain Hembree was killed at the first fire.

He was scalped, stripped, and all personal valuables taken while his hapless comrades looked on. Among the items taken from his body was the official tally of Co. E on the proposed constitutional convention. The company's final vote was never formally entered because of this irreplaceable loss.

The Volunteers, once recovered from their astonishment, labored furiously to inflict some stinging hurt on the attackers. Their efforts were foredoomed by worn-out horses that made impossible any effective pursuit. Even so, it was claimed a few days later that "we killed ten or twelve Indians," although the diary mentions only two killed in separate skirmishes.[104]

The Volunteers, by this juncture, were probably uninterested in any accurate assessment of victories or futile chases. Most were consumed by an uncomplicated yearning for food and a military discharge. Cornelius estimated that the regiment "has eaten about one hundred of indians horses." To make fun of the vain wanderings of the command between March 9 and April 16, 1856, is to smirk at a harrowing ordeal for the marchers. One letter recounted that, "We was near 6 weeks living on horse meat . . . and before we got in we was nearly all afoot we have eat our horses we lived on prickly pares and wild onions for about a week before we got in to the settlements to save a few horses for the sick to ride." Less appetizing were "badgers, dogs, and poor broke-down steers and cows" that some ate. It was true that there was not "enough to eat since we left camp Cornelius" and for five days preceding the Canyon Creek battle the men "lived upon horse flesh and coffee," with no sugar, and half rations of flour.[105]

The Volunteers waited at Five Mile Camp from April 13 to 30, while Cornelius was at The Dalles pushing for provisions and decisions about the future. A full week before the skirmish on Canyon Creek, he insisted that "several instances of mismanagement have occurred in the quarter masters department in the field, that have seriously embarrassed my plans and movements." Harsher still was the charge that "the head of the quartermaster department in the field has either willfully or ignorantly neglected his duty." Co. C, Recruiting Battalion, was actually out of food for a full day. This probably accounts for Ankeny's grim prophecy that many would die "from the carelessness and incompetency on the part of the Quartermasters and Commissaries . . . in the valley and at The Dalles, for not forwarding necessaries of life to sustain the command in the field."[106]

Curry's response to these biting censures was baffling. He reminded John McCracken, assistant quartermaster general, that "it is highly desirable to avoid every just cause of complaint . . . arising from inadequacy or uncertainty of supplies." On the same day, April 12, he admitted that "our service has been subjected to many unavoidable embarrassments from defective arrangements in the departments of supply and subsistence." Some of these very words were used in Cornelius' protest against the inefficiency of the Commissary and Quartermaster departments. Yet, a few days later, Curry didn't blush to tell the Colonel that

> I am assured by the chiefs of the Commissary and Quartermaster Departments that there has not been any time since the troops have been in the field such an insufficiency of supplies of any sort as to retard much less paralyse their movements, had they been prudently and efficiently distributed under the direction of the proper officer.

A separate letter on the same day, April 16, assured Kelly "that there has been at no time an adequate supply there [The Dalles] for the comfortable subsistence of the whole force in the field." When Curry tried similar tactics on Nesmith months before, he triggered that colonel's resignation.[107]

These mealy-mouthed, temporizing evasions were no more effective with Cornelius, who demanded a formal court of inquiry which was refused by Curry for reasons explained orally but never written. This contemptible try to blame long-suffering Cornelius was branded as "wrong & will recoil on the heads of those who lend themselves to the dissemination of any such imputation against Col. Cornelius. The sole fault rests on Curry & on the QM & C in the field."[108]

These uniformly caustic charges by every experienced Volunteer belatedly goaded the Governor into sending M. M. McCarver, Quartermaster General,

> to the Dalles to give your personal attention to the wants of the Volunteers, and see what can be done towards speedily relieving their necessities, answering their complaints, and making such ample provision for them in your line as may be requisite to again prepare them for the field.

Long-time promoter McCarver manifested greater realism and prudence as he dwelt more on the possibility of imminent discharge than any return to battle. He coped adroitly with the constant absence of food when "He said that he had the books to show that he had purchased full rations for the Regiment untill the first of June. He could not say who was to blame for it not being forwarded to us."

50

And three weeks later his published explanation was that "The duty of the Commissary General is to purchase the Subsistence for the army, and to notify the Quarter-Masters department of that fact; *whose* duty alone it is, to have it transported to the army.[109] When this self-exonerating apologia appeared in the press, nearly all of the men were safely at home recuperating and trying to erase distasteful memories.

Much of the high-level maneuvering was mostly rumored among the veterans waiting impatiently at Five Mile Camp. They were actually only a few days away from "getting discharged," but they were without word. When notification did come, the unbeaten foe blunted their elation with a parting humiliation.

The Indians' farewell mocking gesture came at seven in the morning, April 28, when they ran off 500 horses before the eyes of the milling horse guard. One audacious dash swept away this achingly assembled solitary evidence of success. Truly, now they were empty handed! Desperate Volunteers pursued on foot, "but did not succeed in retaking the horses, so were all left afoot." Farrar admitted openly that "It is a devil of a *lick* to us; Kamiakin is playing a strong hand. The old fellow got about 100,000$ worth of property out of us before breakfast."[110]

This final jibe, almost within sight of The Dalles, far excelled a similar dash near Fort Henrietta in the previous week. There, the Indians killed and scalped Lot Holinger, one of the horse guard, while driving "off all of the horses of Co. B & those of the wagon master & also" Kelly's personal mount.[111] These daredevil attacks were the flamboyant finish to a prolonged, harsh inconclusive search for a still unfettered enemy.

The grueling winter in the field, supporters always maintained, was designed to keep the Indians moving and furnish a protective screen for the settlers. This need vanished with the definite departure of Wright's U.S. infantrymen for the Yakima country, April 28, 1856. Curry ordered the withdrawal of the Volunteers from the north side of the Columbia, this same day. There was, too, the real impossibility of further detaining the underfed, undisciplined, and restless civilian soldiers.[112]

Wright's presence in the Yakima country left that of the Walla Wallas unoccupied and unpoliced. Curry retained his original conviction that armed forces should be stationed among the Walla Wallas until U.S. or Washington territorial units assumed permanent responsibility. Kelly was asked to persuade Co. K, under Rivais, to *volunteer* for this duty. The hardened campaigners for the first time

51

declined an assignment. The task devolved, then, upon newly organized companies of Oregon Mounted Rangers that served from May 15 to Aug. 21, 1856.[113]

Governor Curry's formal recall of the Volunteers was acted upon with commendable speed. The spent companies gathered at the designated rendezvous points where they were rapidly discharged. Those on the south side of the Columbia, as Cason's Co. E, Recruiting Battalion, looked for Indians and horses during their return. French Prairie's Co. K delivered 200 horses to the Willamette Valley before mustering out at Salem. Co. A, with Plympton Kelly, boarded the *Wasco* May 1, and arrived across the Willamette from Portland, May 3, after delay by winds and a transfer to the *Fashion* at the Cascades.[114]

> No heroes' welcome awaited them. The newly arrived Volunteers look as if they had seen hard times during the campaign. They are poor in flesh, pale and haggard in appearance and far from being decently or comfortably clad. Neither Gov Curry or his officials are here to welcome back these men who have encountered untold dangers and hardships during the winter for the protection of the country.[115]

The barrage of complaints over the chronic shortage of supplies may have dissuaded Curry from facing the underfed veterans.

# Biography of
# Plympton J. Kelly

Plympton J. Kelly was 20 years old when he came to Oregon in 1848. His father, Clinton, brought him, his brothers, Hampton and Archon, with the rest of the family from Kentucky. The elder Kelly, a tireless Methodist preacher, became profoundly disheartened when the church divided into Northern and Southern jurisdictions over slavery. The gloomy prospect of continued work in the afflicted state impelled him to move to Oregon where he hoped no poisonous prejudices tainted the frontier settlers.

Eleven members of the family left Kentucky in the fall of 1847, wintered at Independence, Missouri, and set out for Oregon May 1, 1848. Four other families and Clinton's brother, Thomas, were in the 12 wagons that reached Oregon City Oct. 2, 1848. This first winter the younger boys, Calmet and Benjal, died. The other sons worked at scoring lumber for George Abernethy, Oregon City's pioneer merchant. The family wasn't really settled until April 1849, when their father selected a 640-acre claim some three miles southeast of Portland. The remaining sons took an active part with their father in the work of developing this property.

The different sons, as time passed, settled in the general vicinity of Powell Valley, across the Willamette from Portland. Plympton, the eldest son, worked along with the family before starting out for himself by filing on a 320-acre donation claim, about five miles east of Portland, December 1850. He built a log cabin and cleared his land until there were some 200 rich acres. Three years later, 1853, he was among the proponents of a new county for the land north and east of the Clackamas River. Along with other relatives and friends on the

53

Willamette's east bank, he petitioned, 1853, for the abrogation of James B. Stephens' ferry monopoly. He went so far as to operate his father's flatboat *Independence* until Stephens overcame this competition by introducing steam on his ferry in 1856.

When Governor George Curry called for volunteers Oct. 11, 1855, to avenge the plundering and slaying of whites by hostile Yakima, Walla Walla and Cayuse Indians, he hastened to enlist in Co. A, First Regiment, Oregon Mounted Volunteers, under command of Capt. Alfred V. Wilson. He began his diary on Nov. 22, 1855 (thereby omitting the first 40 days of his service) and closed with his arrival at home May 3, 1856, a day marred by "one of the worst chills I ever had in my life."

A few days proved that he was not one "that will never risk themselves far from home any more after they get out of this."[116] He served in Co. K, 9th Regiment, Oregon Mounted Volunteers (Rangers) from May 8 to June 16, 1856, under Capt. W. S. Buckley. He kept no diary of this second tour that put him among the first to enlist and the last to come home.

Several years later he collected a total of $91.15 for his service in both companies. This sum helped not at all when he came home from the war and needed money. Scattered notes, on unused places in the diary book, disclose considerable work for his father and several loans of wheat or money from this dependable source. Each transaction in the winter-spring, 1856-1857, was carefully noted as the veteran resumed management of his affairs. He was temporarily diverted from farming during the year 1858-1859, when he operated the riverboat *Multnomah*, largely as a livestock carrier from the Cascades and Oregon City to the mouth of the Columbia River.[117]

Plympton had been in Oregon 15 years, owned his farm for 14 of these, and was 35 years old when he married Elizabeth Clark July 4, 1864. Only three of their six children, Eudoxia, Mary and James, lived into adulthood to gladden their parents' 42 years of marriage.

Clinton Kelly's many years of personal dedication to the Methodist church were reflected in his children. Although never resuming his former role of official pastor, he was always vigorously active in the church in Oregon. Small wonder, then, that Plympton and Hampton were united on probation with Portland's First Methodist Church in the fall of 1849, a few months after reaching Oregon City. Plympton in due time became a licensed exhorter and conducted services, whenever asked, throughout his life. He was a faithful superintendent of Sunday School for almost 40 years. This life-long loyalty and devotion to church suffused his closing years with a patriarchal aura.

He was increasingly revered, too, as a surviving pioneer of Oregon. There was even an appropriateness about his final illness. His last reasonably normal day, about a month before his death, saw him spend several hours of a Sunday discussing early Oregon history with George H. Himes, Portland printer and historian. The probable strain of this long session may have occasioned the stroke suffered after his visitor's departure. He lingered nearly a month prior to his death Sept. 15, 1906.

Two days later a large crowd of relatives and friends attended the funeral service of not the oldest, not the most famous, not the last, but of a genuine Oregon founder.[118]

*Plympton J. Kelly, Co. A,*
*First Regiment, Oregon Mounted Volunteers*

# Indian War Diary

## November 22, 1855 – May 3, 1856

# John Tully Kerns map 1855

This map from the John Tully Kerns Diary gives an accurate picture of the actual route followed by the Oregon Mounted Volunteer forces. The trail from The Dalles to the Walla Walla Valley was nothing more than the Oregon Trail through modern Miller, Biggs, Rock Creek, Cecil, Well Springs, and Butter Creek to the Umatilla River near Stanfield. The Walla Walla trail angled northeastward from the Umatilla across Cold Springs and Juniper canyons and over the high ridges into the vicinity of Whitman's former mission.

58

Plympton J. Kelly's diary is one of the most extensive and enlightening personal narratives to survive from the Yakima, Walla Walla and Cayuse Indian War in Washington and Oregon territories, October, 1855—May, 1856. It is a spontaneous, contemporary record by an energetic participant in or an alert observer of the stirring action.

The editor has tried to retain the flavor of an unstudied document, while making it more immediately intelligible to a modern reader. All punctuation is introduced with the sole intent of clarifying otherwise confusing passages. The original diary contains not a single punctuation mark.

Captions for the daily entries have been supplied in uniform style by the editor. Kelly usually noted the date and the day without the month except at each new month's beginning.

The author's spellings remain in their pristine form with only an occasional correction placed in conventional brackets to spare the reader needless puzzlement. The diarist consistently spells off as "of" and been as "ben." His unique "of" may require a re-reading but it helps preserve the individuality of the account.

The few conjectural emendations and elucidations in the text are enclosed in brackets.


**NOVEMBER 22, 1855 [Thursday]**  A clear frosty morning getting ready to start for the Walla Walla country.[119] It seems that nothing can be done in a hurry when we are at the Dalles by Company A for between liquor and grumbling we have had a hard time of it at this place. Pack animals are the poorest means of conveying freight that man ever thought of. Traveled 5 miles and camped on a little Creek.[120] This has been a beautiful day for Nov [ember] it has not been warm enough to thaw in the shade. Wood is scarce grass is plenty such as it is.

**NOVEMBER 23rd [Friday]**  A clear frosty morning the wind from the East. Received information that Major Chinn is stopped at the Utilla by the Indians and we have orders to hasten to his relief.[121] We have got material to make tents. Traveled 5 miles camped on the little DesChutes nothing but brush for wood, grass scarce. A pack train came up with us to day a disagreeably cool [one].

**NOVEMBER 24th [Saturday]**  A cloudy morning traveled 5 miles and crossed the DesChutes at its junction with the Columbia River saw a mountain fox or cayota it was nearly white and the size of a smal fist. Traveled 6 miles up the Columbia. The grass being very scarc we turned up a ravine the bottom of wich was very rough owing to the greate number of boulders in it. Watter is found in pudles and holes, ocasionaly as we past up the ravine we could see where small springs brok out of the Mountains surrounded by green grass. By the way, the grass is very scarce from the fact that the grass has ben burnt up the passt season. Camped 2½ miles up the ravine from the Columbia. Water wood and grass better than could have ben expected owing to the forbidding appearance of the country. The day [has] ben clear and cool.

**NOVEMBER 25th Sunday.**   Went up the ravine about a mil and came to the Imigrant Roade. The Rode passed throu roling prarie covered with dry bunch grass where it had not been burnt of. Traveled 21 miles crossed John days River 3 miles up Alder Creek and camped. Grass scarce wood and water plenty. The banks of this creek are lined with Alder. This creek has been known by the names of Rock an [d] Cedar Creek. We heard that the Indians promised to give us battle on friday next. This day has been cloudy and cold.

**NOVEMBER 26th Monday.**   This morning we elected Wm Baily 2nd Sargent. Liutenant Col Kelly came with our Company this morning. Traveled 3 miles up Alder Creek and camped the grass is scarce along this creek the country which we traveled is rough and barren in appearance the soil is too sandy to produce well. This is a pleasant day.

**NOVEMBER 27th Tuesday.**   This has been a tolerable pleasant day. The country through which we travel to day is very near barren there [is] nothing to be seen but sage [a] scatering of bunch grass and here and there a fiew scrub Cedars. The soil is almost entirely sand the surface of this country would be a drifting sand if it were not for the little weedes and grass that grow on its surface. Traveled 25 miles Camped on Willow Creek. There is more evidence here of the hardships of the Imigration to Oregon than I ever saw before the bones of cattle, wagon irons and 16 graves they all appear to have ben mad in 1852.[122] Grass and wood tolerabli plenty watter rather scarce.

**NOVEMBER 28th Wensday.**   The country throug which we traveled to day is about the same as yesterday so far as the soil and vegitation is concerned. The face of the country is not so broken as that of yesterday. I noticed on the left a long line of Juniper trees. Camped at the well spring the watter of this spring is slightly warm it is slightly coffee coloured. Traveled 10 miles. No wood here but sage and Juniper. Grass scarce. A disagreably windy day driving dust and sand about furiously.

**NOVEMBER 29th [Thursday]**   A cloudy day a few drops of rain in the evening. The country about the same as yesterday. After crossing butter creek we noticed a smoke on the Utilla below where we expected to find Major Chinn. We left the Road to our right and traveled in the direction of the smok but the prickly pairs wer so disagreeable to our horses feete as to caused us to turn about to the Road.[123] The smoke was past or at the same time some concluded that it had ben raised by the Indians to give notice that we wer coming. This is the Indian mode of informing each other of the approach of an enemy. Major Chinn command was not aware of our coming till they saw two fires at two different places on the Mountains last night which was a sign that two Companies wer coming.[124] This signal was noticed in regard to the approach of Captain Munsons company. We reache[d] Major Chinn encamped on the utilla and found that he had built a picket fort with two bastion. It is somewhat difficult to say whether such precaution was necessary or not if reports be true it is not. The simple fact is Major Chinn is a shrewed Lawyer but no warior. It seems that Volunteers have commited a greate blunder in electing theire Field officers for evry one that has had an opportunity to prove himself has lacked that courage and bravery so necessary in a military Commander. Wood and watter abundant grass scarce owing more to the fact that it has been eaten up than the poverty of the soil fo [r] in my opinion the soil is fertile along the bottom of this River. We wer received by the Companies at this place with all the demonstrations of joy that they wer capable of. Indeed they appear to be men that would do themselves and country an honor if they had the man to leade them to the field of battle.

**NOVEMBER 30th Friday.**   Rained last night and raining to day till noon. This has been one of [the] windiest days I ever saw it blowed down the tents in spite of all we could do we had to go to the bush in the evening to cook our grub. Thomas Kelly in company with several others went down the River 3 or 4 miles and found several Indian Cashes that had been broken open by the Volunteers before one of which contained potatoes a fiew of which I saw·they wer fine the other contained Camus bred Root it was a good substitute for bread.

*Site of Fort Henrietta, looking South. Fort at the left.*     Vance Colburn
Oregon Historical Society

Thomas Kelly brought some Camuse B[r]ead Root and one cake of the Bread to camp. The Volunteers have taken [17] horses and one cow of the Indians a fiew days ago. This fort is on the same ground that the agency buildings stood on before they wer burnt by the Indians.

**DECEMBER 1, 1855. [Saturday]**   This is a pleasant day. A general inspection of arms was had to-day and distribution of ammunition. All the beef has ben issued to-day that is on hand so we will have to make a drive on the Indians before we get anymore shortly. Thi[s] morning an express was sent to the Dalls for more provision.

**DECEMBER 2nd Sunday.**   Snowing this morning. All hand [s] making preparations to March for fort Walla Walla to night. In the evening it cleared up. We wer all ready to March an hour after dark except 25 men who wer left as a guard to the Fort. The fore part of the night was clear and cold without any wind about Midnight the sky became hazy and the wind arose it was not possible to keep warm without walking. the Country through which we travled in the fore part of the Night was a level plain with a fiew depressiones and elevations Some

63

parts of which was covered with dry bunch grass and others bare the cause of wich I could not tell whether it was fire or sterility of soil. About Midnight we went up in a ravine from that time till daylight we wer sometimes in ravines and sometimes on the tops of Mountains. The ground was froze hard. The grass has been burnt up. The ground seemed as if some farmer had fed hogs on the ground such I frequently fancied as we ascended the hills that I could see some old farm building with a line of fence near it such was the illusion caused by the darkness and sleepy eyes. I lost my cartridge box. It is very difficult for a large body of men to travel together in the night without[t] getting separated where they have no roade one time during the night the regiment came very near being separated. Daylight found us in a deep ravine instead of being round the fort not knowing exactly where we wer it was not the fault of the guide altogether for he had ben trying to pick a way for a wagon we had along it was designed for a hospital wagon.[125]

**About sunrise DECEMBER 3rd [Monday]** it commenced snowing then turned to rain. I have not often endured more suffering than I have on this march. About 10 o'clock we came to Walla Walla River and forded it. We camped half mile below the ford our animals had ben saddled for 18 hours. We have not seen or heard of any Indians during our march. We got our breakfast and all who wished to started for the fort which was said to be a mile and a half distant from our camp but when we came to travel it is proved to be three.[126] Those who got there first advanced with some caution till they saw the Crows flying and alighting on the buildings. We entered the Fort and found that it had ben robed of every thing that was of any importance to the Indians. The floores of the buildings had ben broken up to see if there was not deposits of goods under them. This fort was built by the Hudson Bay Company but is now the property of Mr. Sinclare. He estimates loss at twenty thousand dollars one item of this loss is a thousand pairs of Blankets.[127] Mr. Sinclare left his Fort at the first outbreak of the Indians. He came back with us. The fort and all the buildings are made of adoboie or unburnt brick the roofs of the buildings are first a layer of split timber than mortar into which straw has ben well worked. There has ben something done in the way of farming the soil looks well.

**DECEMBER 4th Tuesday.** It was reported in camp this morning that 25 Indians wer crossing the Columbia River near the fort. All those that wished too [left] for the fort in hopes of getting a fight with

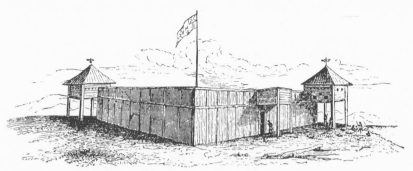

FORT WALLAWALLA.

Sketches made in 1841 by a member of the Wilkes' expedition. The bastions on the corners were used by the Whitmans and the Spaldings as bedrooms when they arrived in September, 1836.

"Fort Wallawalla is about two hundred feet square, and is built of pickets, with a gallery or staging on the inside, whence the pickets may be looked over. It has two bastions, one on the southwest and the other on the northeast. On the inside are several buildings, constructed of logs and mud; one of these is the Indian store; the whole is covered with sand and dust, which is blown about in vast quantities."

Wilkes, *The United States Exploring Expedition, 1838-1842*, Vol. IV, pp. 390-391.

Oregon Historical Society

the Indians. They found the Indians on the oposite side of the River with there provisions deposited on the Bank of the River. The volunteers waded a slough in order to get as near the Indians as possible. They fired at the Indians across the River it being 400 yards wide. They had no means of crossing it but a canoe so they did not attempt it. They believ that they killed one Indian. It was reported about noon in camp that the Indians wer advancing to atact the [camp]. After considerable bustle and confusion the scouting parties wer sent out to see where the Indians wer. We found them on the top of a hill 3 miles up the River. There was perhaps forty of them. We found our horses too weak to come up with them. We followed them 3 or 4 miles but never could get nearer than 4 or 5 hundred yards. We fired a fiew shots at them and once they returned it the balls passing close to us. In the evening we discovered that they wer driving of cattle so it was thought necessary to send back for more men. On the way back we met Major Chinn on his way out accompanied by Nathan Olney the Indian agent. When they came near the Indians Olney caled to them and invited them to send some one to talk with him. After receiving asurances that they would not be hurt they sent three to talk with him. They told him that the Cayuses wer still friendly toward the whites.

**DECEMBER 5th Wensday.**   A cloudy morning. The Companies have selected all there best horses to pursue the enemy. And those men who have not good horses are to gard the baggage train crossed the Walla Walla River and directe [d] our course to the Tushe River. As we wer descending the hills to the Tushe we discovered a band of cattle a welcom sight to us for our beef cattle wer getting dangerously thin. The country through which we traveled to day is broken covered with bunch grass in places and in others with sage and greese wood.[128] We encamped on the Tushe. Grass plenty such as it is for it is dry. Poor wood. The number of cattle taken to day 47 head by the baggag train. It commenced raining about sundown and after dark it snowed. About half past 6 o clock an express arrived in camp from Col Kelly to Major Chinn calling for 75 men as old peu peu Mox Mox had come into the regiment with a white flag accompanied by 40 of his wariors. He wished to have a talk with the Whites and invited Col Kelly and command to go to his camp. The Col thought it propper to surround them with a guard for the night and expects to ask terms of peace that the Indians will not comply with without a fight hence the reason for wanting reenforcements.

**DECEMBER 6th Thursday**  A very disagreeable morning. We started early for Col Kelly's command. We traveled over a very broken country passt 3 old Indians encampment. About 1 o clock we came with Col K command at an Indian encampment where they wer engaged in a council with peu peu Mox Mox. The terms of peace offered him by Col K is that he give up his arms amunition and stock that he is not likly to comply with if he wer at liberty for himself and 5 of his wariors are prisoners. His wariors are on the hill around us but refuse to come in and surrender there arms. We started for our camp about 3 o clock. We took a much shorter way to camp than that [by which] we came. The country throug wich we returned [is covered] with a fine growth of bunch grass. We got to camp after dark. After going to bed one of the prisoners tryed to get away by springing out of bed but was caught by the guard after which they wer all tied.

**DECEMBER 7th Friday.**  This morning the Indians apeared on the high ground on the oposit side of the River. They said that they did not want us to advance any further into there country for they said that there young men would hurt us if we advanced further into there country. As soon as we got ready we crossed the Tushe. The Indians fell back and as Companies B H and I advanced to the high ground the Indians fired on them.[129] The Companies halted for a short time then they charged [the] enemy and they fled up the Walla Walla valley the Volunteers pursuing them several miles when the Indians made a

66

*Gate of the Columbia as seen from Ft. Walla Walla, 1854.*

stand at the French Farms below Whitmans station. They took to [the] brush and fought obstantly but wer driven out of the brush with great loss on there part and the Volunteers had killed Captain Bennet Liutenant Burris and E. B. Kelso and others wer wounded at the same time.[130] The Indians made several resol [ute] charges upon us on the hills but wer successfully repulsed. The Indians took possession of a farm house and stock yard from which they could not be easily driven.[131] Captain Wilson got a small howitzer that we brought from fort Walla Walla and fired on them 3 times at the fourth fire the gun burst and seriously [injured] the Capt.[132] The firing had no other effect on them than to scare them. The Indians would not come nearer to us than 3 or 4 hundred yard in the open prarie. At night we fell back to a farm house in our rear where the wounded and dead had ben collected and where the pack train had stoped. The 5 prisoners wer kiled at this place as they refused to be tied. After dark a couple of shots wer fired into the camp at which the fires wer put out and the men paraded and posted in the fence line for the night. The Indians wer encamped at the upper farm house. They set fire to the oats and straw stack.

67

**DECEMBER 8th Saturday.** The Indians made there apearance early in the morning. There was some hot fighting to day. Jesse Flemming was mortally wounded in the evening. Nothing has been done to day in the way of driving the Indians from there position. The Col commenced [to] fortify our camp by pickets and ditches. There has been found deposits of potatoes corn and wheat at this place.

**DECEMBER 9th. Sunday.** The Indians made there appeara[nc]e earlly as usual. They have tried to day to scare us of by yelling and screaming. They effected but little by it. Last night an express was started for fort Henrietta and the Dalls. Our amunition is getting low. There has ben a considerable quantity of corn packed up from below.

**DECEMBER 10th Monday.** Anothe[r] days fight before us. The Indians have been routed on all points. To Day about Noon a signal smoke was noticed on the bluff on the oposit side of the River which gave us hopes that reenforcements wer coming and in the evening the Washington County company and part of the Yamhill Company came to our relief with a good supply of amunition whic was very much needed.[133] The Indians appear to be disheart[en]ed.

**DECEMBER 11th Tuesday.** No Indians in sight. All the men are ordered to be mounted that can find horses. The Washington and Yamhill companies wer sent up the reight side of the River. [The] ballance of the command went up on the left some on the bottom near the timber and some on the hills. The footmen went up as far as the Indian encampment. When the horsemen pursued on the trail of the Indians which was very large the Indians followed Mill creek they took the trail to Colvill. We crossed over to dry Creeke where we met a fiew N[ez] Perce Indians with a letter from Raymo a frenchman requesting us to protect him and others who had fled to the Nez Perces for protection from the Walla Walla valey the letter stating that they wer now at Chases Claim on the Tushe. Liutenant Col Kelly sent them an answer that he would come [to] there relief. We went on to the Copei and camped after dark. We killed two cows and two calves as we had brought nothing with us to eate so we had to eat Roast beeff without salt a poor show for a living. We have seen a good many Indian horses and Cattle. From the signs the Indians have left in a hurry and if we had fresh horses we could overtake them but as it is we can only scare them and pick up what stock they have left. The country through which we travled to day is as fine a country for

68

Peu-Peu-Mox-Mox.
Head Chief of the Walla Walla Indians.

Agricultural or grazing purposes as I ever seen the only drawback is the want of timber.

**DECEMBER 12th Wensday.**   This morning Company K was sent to the relief of the French.[134] The ballance of the command went down the creek to the Tushe a part of the command crossed over and went up to Bomford ['s] improvement.[135] We found the house burned this is said to have been worth a thousand dollars there was found two trunks that wer left by Mr. Bomford containing clothing trinkets and Books. I got a volume of Dannas Minerology.[136] We drove all the cattle and horses back to our camp on the Copei more cattle slaughtered and more roast beef without salt.

**DECEMBER 13th Thursday.** It snowed last night. A gloomy morning. We start for the camp we drove in all the cattle and horses we could find. Jesse Flemming died this evening.

**DECEMBER 14th Friday.** Buried Jesse Flemming this morning. It rained last night. Major Chinn and Captain Wilson went to look for a new camping place. This place has become a perfect hog hole for mud. There is enough of beef entrails and dead Indians lying around this place to bread a pestilence if the weather wer warm enough. Yesterday peu peu Mox Mox was taken up by Dr. Shaw and his ears cut of and to day he has ben taken out and subject to further indignities.[137] Sargent Roberts found a hand mill on which we grind our corn and wheat and we have not drawn any flour for several days and sugar is not to [be] had at present but we have corn wheat potatoes and peas and Beef and pork.[138] We heard to day that the hostile [Indians] have dispersed themselves over the country. They report there loss as being only two but we know it to be from 75 to 100 killed and wounded.

**DECEMBER 15th Saturday.** A cloudy morning. We are to move camp to day. After a greate deal of hunting horses we got under way. We passed Whitmans old station its former glory is gone nothing but a part of an adobie wall a part of the grist mill and a fiew embankment[s] is all that is left to remind the traveler that here once lived the Indians greatest friend.[139] The place is too flat and low to be admired. We pitched our camp 2 miles above the station the ground is very good for an encampment wood is not as abundant as could be desired grass abundant.[140] There is a farm on the opposite sid of the Creek at which some wheat was found and a fiew hogs.

**DECEMBER 16th Sunday.** A cloudy frosty morning. The rolls of the different companies wer called this morning and the whole command paraded and Major Chinn delivered the general rules for the com-

*Desolate butte at Wallula.*  Washington State Historical Society

mand. First he congratulated us on our victory over the Indians. He also informed us that the French settlers would return to there farms in a fiew days accompanied by those friendly Indians who protected them and that we should respect there persons and property.[141] 2 that no more cashes should be raised but by the men in the service of the Commissary. 3 that no more hogs be killed. 4 that there be no more stealing.

**DECEMBER 17th Monday.** It snowed last night. This morning things look very gloomy. A good deal [of] dissatisfactio [n] is on account of the way the Commissary conducts his department.[142] He has some flour still on hand but has not issued any for a week there is some talk of taking it by force and dividing it. At about 9 o clock the sun shone out and the snow went of rapidly. The after part of the day has ben beautiful. This evening it was reported in camp that Nathan Olney and others wer driving of a large number of horses Liutenant Wright and 10 men went in pursuit of them with orders to bring them back.

71

**DECEMBER 18th Tuesday.** A cloudy morning about cold enough to frieze. It seems that if we cannot find Indians to fight we will have fights among ourselves. The Commissary this morning told a man that he was a thief the man in turn thought that the Commissary needed a drubing for such talk and would have given it to him if no on[e] had have interfered. After having a cloudy day we had a fine sunset it showed to greate advantage on the snowy mountains around us. This day has been pleasantly warm.

**DECEMBER 19th Wensday.** It rained last night. An Express came in from the Dalls last night by which we learned that Col Nesmith had resigned.[143] Lieutenant Col Kelly informed us at roll call that there was to be an election for Colonel this evening at three o clock and he himself had determined to return to the valey and take his place in the legislature and he promises to do all he can for us as the governor has refered the war affairs to the Legislature to be disposed of by that [body] as they think best.[144] We also have the promise of a small supply of flour to day with the prospect of a full supply in a fiew days. The promised supply of flour when it came was but 50 pounds to the Company. The candidates for Colonel wer Captain Layton of Linn County and Captain Cornelius of Washington County. The latter was elected. The sick and wounded started for the Dalls this evening accompanied by the wagons. They also carry bak the remains of Captain Bennet.

**DECEMBER 20th Thursday.** Last night the wind was very high. This morning it is very warm for this season of the year. About noon it was announced in camp that governor Stevens and party were close by.[145] Orders wer given for all the men in camp to be paraded with there arms. We had hardly time to get to our places when him and party came in sight. The howitzer sent forth the first salute then the small arms and howitzer agane then the Nez Perces fired a salute in return then three cheers for governor Stevens which was returned by the Indians. They had a sort of drum on which they beat to the sound of which several sang and kept time the musick was of the rudest kind. Three voleys wer fired by the small arms accompanied by a greate deal of cheer[ing] by all parties. After the cheering and firing was over the Volunteers wer formed in a hollow square when Col Cornelius introduced governor Stevens to us. The governor told us that this was a hapy day for him and his party. He said that we wer not summer soldiers that snow mountains and ice bound Rivers had no terrors for us. He said last June when he left this valley evry Indian

*Crossing the Bitter Root mountains Nov. 1855*

*Governor I.I. Stevens' Party enroute to Olympia.*   Washington State Historical Society

here took him by the hand and said there heart [s] wer good toward the white man. They said that they had doubts heretofore as to the course they should pursue in regard to the whites but now it was all right. He said I went on my way to the Blackfoot council little thinking that those who had promised to be faithful to me would be up in arms against the whites. He told us that he set out on his return from fort Benton with 25 men and them but half armed and only forty rounds of amunition. When they wer met by a man who informed him of the hostile attitude of the Indians when he returned and armed his whole party and got 10000 rounds of amunition and a fresh supply of horses. They crossed the Rocky Mountains and bitter Root Mountains with out any accident befalling them. They wer met in the spokan valley by the Nez Perces who said that there hearts wer still good and wer ready to help him punish those who had proved treacherous. He also found at the same place 25 miners from Colvill who

73

offered him there services which he accepted and mustered them into the service of the Territory. He came on to the Nez Perce country when the Indians offered to a man to accompany him on his way but he told them that the better half of them had best remain at home so only 75 came with him. He also informed us that those Indians who had lately ben engaged with us in battle wer scatered from the mouth of snake River up to the mouth of two Cannon in a disorganized state part of there stock on this side of the River and part on the other side. He thinks that the hostile Indians can bring into the field from 6 to 8 hundred warriors. His advice is that the campaign be prosecuted with vigor through this winter for if it is not settled before the snows melt in the mountains they will escap to the Buffalo country and mak mischief with other Indian tribes that are now friendly.

**DECEMBER 21st Friday.**   Raining this morning. About noon to day it was reported in camp that some persons wer driving of horses and as many men as could find their horses started in pursuit. It commenced snowing this evening. A fiew pack mules wer started for fort Henrietta for provision. About 8 o clock those who went to look after the horse thieves got back to camp they did not find the thieves or there trail.

**DECEMBER 22nd Saturday.**   A gloomy morning the snow 6 inches deep it has not snowed any to day.

**DECEMBER 23rd Sunday.**   The thermometer was 19 degrees below zero this morning. We can do nothing but get wood and cook.

**DECEMBER 24th Monday.**   This morning the thermometer is 21 degrees below zero. A horse and mule died or froze to death last night a gloomy prospect for our poor animals.

**DECEMBER 25th Tuesday.**   Christmas as cold as the past two days.

**DECEMBER 26th Wensday.**   A cold cloudy day.[146]

**DECEMBER 27th Thursday.**   It is a little warmer. This evening two men came to camp and reported 20 pack animals at wild horse creek with provisions.

**DECEMBER 28th Friday.**   The pack train sent to fort Henrietta for provision got back this evening and brought 800 pounds of flour seven

*Isaac I. Stevens, Territorial Governor, Superintendent of Indian Affairs.*

*Looking-Glass, Chief of the Nez Perce.*

shirts and two pair of pants for each Company and 100 pounds of tobacco.

**DECEMBER 29th Saturday.** I went up to camp this morning and was sent with out [delay to drive] in horses. I found some of them in tolerable good condition and some hardly able to get along the prospec[t] is gloomy indeede for our poor animals if this snow does not melt of shortly.

**DECEMBER 30th Sunday.** A cold day there is no prospect of the snow melting of yet. We have heard nothing from below as yet.

**DECEMBER 31st Monday.** Snowing this morning not so cold as it has ben.

**JANUARY 1, 1856. [Tuesday]** It has ben cloudy all day. Yesterday Mr. Sinclare with some of the volunteers started for fort Walla Walla. They saw 15 hostile Indians. They turned back. They suppose that the fort is occupied by the Yacama Indians. Major Chinn has issued a written order against taking Indian horses the cause why this order was given was that some of th[e] men wer medling with the horses of the friendly Indians.[147]

**JANUARY 2nd Wensday.** Snowing this morning. It has ben cloudy all day a little warmer than it has ben. Potatoes and beef is our living now and I think in 12 days there will be no potatoes. This evening Adjutant Farrar Joseph Meek and a pack train from the Dalls with provision. Thomas Kelly came with them.

**JANUARY 3rd Thursday.** It is thawing this morning a welcome sight to us. We have drawn flour to day the first some of us have drawn for near three weeks.

**JANUARY 4th Friday.** The wind blowed very hard last night the snow is melting very fast this morning. To day Col Cornelius takes command of the regiment. A pack train started for Henrietta.[148]

**JANUARY 5th Saturday.** The wind blowed pretty hard last night the snow is all most gone. 25 men wer sent out [to] hunt up the horses of the regiment. They found more horses alive than I had expected but ther is not many of them fit for service.

**JANUARY 6th Sunday.** A pleasant morning. We are to move camp to day. We are encamped on Mill Creek above wher the trail leaves the Creek for snak River our [camp] is on an island. Wood and grass plenty.[149]

**JANUARY 7th Monday.** The ground is frozen and the sky is cloudy. It commenced snowing about 5 o clock about sundown it ceased the snow is about 1 inch deepe. The timber on th[e] blue Mountains is in sight all covered with snow.

**JANUARY 8th Tuesday.** The country around presents wintery prospect yet it is not very cold. The Commissary department got up from the lower camp.

**JANUARY 9th Wensday.** A cold disagreeable morning. I was sent out to hunt for beef cattl went out to the foot of the blue Mountains and found but four head. We passed over some of as fine land as I eve[r] saw. Found no snow on the high ground the grass was better than any I have [seen] lately. There is a goo[d] deal of grumbling in camp for beef is gett[ing] scarc and we have but littl else to eat and the prospect is very poor for the future.

**JANUARY 10th Thursday.** A frosty morning about 9 o clock the fog rose as it has done for several days past. There was a party of men sent down to the Tushe to look after some Indians and horses reported to be there. Some men have ben sent out to day [to] drive in beef cattle they drove in a young cow and killed another a[nd] brought the hind quarters of it.

**JANUARY 11th Friday.** A clear morning and a beautiful sunrise but at the appointed [hour] the fog covered the whole face of the country. Captain Wilson started with a pack train for Henrietta for provision the prospect is getting very gloomy in reguard to something to eat if we do not have better success in finding beef cattle things will soon be desparate with us. After dark Captain Embry and Liutenant Hardin got in to camp they have ben out toward snake River they saw no Indians and found but little stock they drove in two cows and 2 caves and a fiew horses.

**JANUARY 12th Saturday** A cool morning. There has ben 2 Bulls drove into camp to day for beef. A fiew men have gone below to get potatoes. Lieutenant Hardin has started to the Dalls on furlough. This has ben a clear pleasant day.

**JANUARY 13th Sunday.** A cold frosty foggy morning. Went down to the farm of Mackbain to get potatoes. We returned back by the old camp about dark and found that there had ben plenty of beef cattle drove in to day the men are quite cheerful the effect of an abundance of beef. An expressman got to camp from the governor with letters to

78

*Yum-how-lish, Cayuse Chief.*

adjutant Farrar. Companies H and I have drove up 175 head of horses and have got them in karaal.[150] It has ben foggy all day.

**JANUARY 14th [Monday] A frosty morning.** There is a goo[d] deal of excitement about camp to day in breaking wild horses. There has ben

79

quite a drove of beef cattle drove in to day so there [is] no danger of starving at present. A foggy day.

**JANUARY 15th Tuesday.** A cloudy day. Liutenant Hibler with 30 men started on a scouting party to snake River late this evening. Several men went below to day to hunt potatoes.

**January 16th Wensday.** A cold frosty morning. Nothing of importance has transpired to day. Some of thos persons who went after potatoes came back to day and reported they could find none.

**JANUARY 17th Thursday.** A warm pleasant morning. About noon Dowels pack train arived in camp with provision from the Dalls. It gave new life to the camp as we could once more have full rations of bread and coffee a thing we have not enjoyed since the 13 of November. I went went out this evening to look after the horses. I found them very much scatered. They wer doing well for the grass is about half green. If we could remain at this camp four weeks more and the weather remain as it has ben the last fiew days our horses would be able to do good service.

**JANUARY 18th Friday.** It snowed last night. It is sufficient to make the grass all white this morning. Mr. Dowel the pack master is in camp and is going [to] start to Portland this evening.

**JANUARY 19th Saturday.** Snowed last night. About 1 o clock to day the pack train that went with Captain Wilson to fort Henrietta got back.

**JANUARY 20th Sunday.** A cloudy morning about 9 o clock the sun showne out cloudy in the evening. Another drove of beef cattle brought [in] this evening they wer found down near fort Walla Walla.

**JANUARY 21st Monday.** Last night Mr. Lansdale got into camp he has ben out with Captain Hembrey on a scout to snake River. He reports a large encampment of Indians at the junction of said River with the Columbia River and they also saw 20 Indians on this side of the River they did not think it prudent to atact them as they kept near the brush. A cloudy morning and quite cold. I started to go to the site of Whitmans saw mill but my companion gave out after going 4 miles so I had to return. We passed by the ruins of two houses one has ben torn down and partly burnt up the other wa[s] fired standing and fire had

80

done nothing but black the logs and burn of the roof. The houses had ben built during the past summer by White men and wer burned by the Indians.

**JANUARY 22nd Tuesday.** Comenced snowing about sun up and snowed till about noon it was about an inch deepe. Major Chinn went over to the French camp to see 4 Indian prisoners who wer taken by Company K. The major returned to camp to day.[151]

**JANUARY 23rd Wensday.** Last night we got up a debate on the question which has done the most to enlighten and civilize the Human race the religion of the Bible or Science. There was considerable interest taken in the debate. During the night there fell two inches of snow this morning cloudy the wind from the south. Captain Embry got back to camp about one o clock to day he brought 250 head of horses.[152] He has ben to the mouth of Snake River. He saw but fiew Indians but he saw the smoke of quite a number of Indian camps aparently behind some timber on the Columbia River. He found no canoe and as he had no means of crossing the River he could find out nothing in regard to the number of the Indians. Snowing this evening.

**JANUARY 24th Thursday.** Snowing this morning. Company E are catching the horses they drove in yesterday. The snow continues 10 inches in depth this evening. An express arived from governor Curry bringing Col Corneliuss commission.[153]

**JANUARY 25th Friday.** The wind from the North a part of the day it was warm enough to thaw.

**JANUARY 26th [Saturday]** A cold morning. Considerable excitement in regard to the election of first Major.

**JANUARY 27th [Sunday]** A light fall of snow last night. I was sent out to day to drive in wild horses. We got the band into the karaal and then the fun commenced of throwing ropes on the horses and dangerous fun it is for if a man should try to hold fast to the rope the skin would be torn from his hands or if he should get entangled in the rope the consequences would be serious but the plan is to throw the rope on and if there is a stump handy they take a turn round it which is likely [to] throw the horse down if this cannot be done the horse is let run til he gets tired then he is choked down and a halter put on. I got a white mare for my labor. Company A has caught several horses to day.

**JANUARY 28th Monday.** Last night the Mill Creek debating Club was organized. To day about 10 o clock Major Chinn got ready to start to the Willamet upon which most of the Volunteers paraded under there colours to hear his farewell adress. The Major said that he had tried to administer justice with an impartial hand and that he had opposed no one knowingly. He said that if he had done any wrong it was of the head and not of the heart. After the Major concluded he received six hearty cheers. Major Chinn has been recalled by governor Curry for what reason we do not know but we have good reason to believe he has ben basely misprisented by some designing persons and [as] the consequence will be elected first Major for we feel inclined to let governor Curry know that he must not remove the officers of our selection if he does not want them raised higher.[154]

**JANUARY 29th Tuesday.** Snowed last night as usual. This morning the command was paraded and the sentence of the Court Martial was read in the cases of Cotenham and Star then the letters of adjutant Barnum and then the governors letter after which the general orders of the Col [were] isued at the conclusion of which three cheers wer given for the Col.[155] The snow is melting to day. There has ben a general driving in of horses to ascertain there condition. There are not many of them fit for effective service.

**JANUARY 30th [Wensday].** A warm pleasant morning foggy. The snow has melted of rapidly to day. Late in the evening this evening an express arived from the Valley bringing letters and papers for the command.

**JANUARY 31st Thursday.** There fell a considerable quantity of snow and rain last night. The snow has melted rapidly. This has ben a windy day. This evening Dowels pack train arrived from fort Henrietta with clothing and provision.

**FEBRUARY 1, 1856 [Friday].** Very windy last night quite warm this morning the snow is melting fast Lieutenant Hannan started for the Dalls to day accompanied by some 20 persons. He is to take the 2 Indian prisoners at the french camp to the Dalls to be retained as prisoners of war.[156]

**FEBRUARY 2nd Saturday.** A frosty morning. About 1 o clock an express from Mr. Craig who resides in the Nez Perce country with a letter stating that Kamiakin the Yacima Chief had joined the hostile

82

Indians on Snake River and that Kamiakins force had ben reenforced by 300 Indians from the coast and that they contemplated crossing the River and attacting us in this valley with a force of some 1000 to 1500. About 2 o clock Mr. Joseph Meek started for Salem bearing letters to the governor.

**FEBRUARY 3rd Sunday.** A cold frosty morning. About 9 o clock the snow commenced falling and continued to fall till 12 o clock and from that time till sundown the country was covered with fogg. At sundown the snow commenced falling again.

**FEBRUARY 4th Monday.** The snow is about 1 inch deepe this morning.

**FEBRUARY 5th Tuesday** A light fall of snow last night. The snow commenced falling about sun up and continued till 2 o clock. The snow is about 4 inches deepe this evening. To day Col Cornelius and Captain Embry started to the Dalls. It was intended this morning that we should move camp to day and the horses wer drove in for that purpose but the snow prevented us from doing so.

**FEBRUARY 6th Wensday.** A frosty morning a clear sunrise. This would be a pleasant day if it wer not for the snow.

**FEBRUARY 7th Thursday.** A frosty morning. We moved camp up the Creek a mile and a half.[157] At this place the Pine timber grows along the margin of the stream. Late in the evening a drove of beef cattle was brought over from the French Camp for we could find no more Indian Cattle in these parts.

**FEBRUARY 8th Friday.** The snow commenced falling about sundown and after dark it rained a while and then snowed. The morning was foggy. This morning a wagon from the French Camp came up with our howitzer and other things which had ben left at Camp Curry.[158]

**FEBRUARY 9th Saturday.** The wind rose very [high] last night and rained quite freely. The snow is pretty nearly all gone.

**FEBRUARY 10th Sunday.** A pleasant morning. A detail of five men was made from each company to build a karaal. Material was sawed out to day with a whip saw to mount our howitzer on. This has ben a pleasant day throughout.

**FEBRUARY 11th Monday.** A beautiful morning. The sun has shone pleasantly all day to day. The hands employed to build boats commenced sawing the lumber to build them.[159]

**FEBRUARY 12th Tuesday.** Last night the guard reported seeing fire above camp and 7 men wer sent up to see what was there but found nothing. There was a slight frost this morning. This has ben a beautiful day.

**FEBRUARY 13th Wensday.** About day break this morning a false alarm was raised by some designing persons. The camp was paraded under arms a diligent search made for Indians but no sign could be found of any Indians. The morning was cloudy and warm about 7 oclock the clouds cleared away and we have had a bright day. This evening our howitzer was tried and we found it would throw shot well.

**FEBRUARY 14th Thursday.** A frosty morning. About noon three men came to camp from the Nez Perce country. They report the hostile Indians encamped in three different encampments and they said the Nez Perce Indians could not be trusted. They say that there has ben several band of stock drove over Snake River lately by Indians professing to be friendly. There has ben a fiew cattle drove in this evening.

**FEBRUARY 15th Friday.** A frosty morning. This morning the Command was paraded under arms to hear the sentence of a court martial.[160] About noon the pack train arived with provision from fort Henrietta.

**FEBRUARY 16th Saturday.** A slight fall of snow this morning. This has been a foggy day. Late this evening three Indian prisoners wer brought over from the French camp.[161]

**FEBRUARY 17th Sunday.** A light fall of snow this morning. Started this morning to escort the pack train to fort Henrietta. We crossed [a] greate many streams. We have traveled [through] some fine country to day. Camped on wild horse Creek. Traveled 25 miles.[162]

**FEBRUARY 18th Monday.** A beautiful morning. We started early from camp the fogg came over soon after leaving camp. The country through which we traveled is a roling prarie the soil apears to be fertile. Camped on the Umatilla River grass scarce. Traveled 20 miles.

84

**FEBRUARY 19th Tuesday.** A cold cloudy morning. Soon after we started the fogg came ove[r] and remained 2 or 3 hours. The Road passed throug a very broken country in fore part of the day the latter part of the [day] passed over a beautiful plain. The soil is not as good [as] that we passed yesterday. Traveled 15 miles and camped on t[he] Umatilla.

**FEBRUARY 20th Wensday.** During the night it rained a little. About sunrise I started down to the fort [Henrietta] 4 miles below. When I got there I found the ox teams had got up from the Dalls with provisions. They will go on to Camp Cornelius. Company A of the 2nd Battalion was camped below the fort.[163] I drew provisions for the escort and returned to camp. Things look very desolate about the fort. The ox teams are camped above us a half mile.[164]

**FEBRUARY 21st Thursday.** A beautiful morning. The packers went down to the fort to get there loads and returned to this camp. Company A of the 2nd battalion is camped one mile above our camp. This has ben a tolerable fine day.

**FEBRUARY 22nd Friday.** A cloudy morning. We have traveled 16 miles to day and are now camped where the Road leaves the Umatilla River for the Walla Walla valey. Grass scarce.

**FEBRUARY 23rd Saturday.** Last night about 11 o clock I went out to see about the horses and [found them] very much scatered. A beautiful morning. We camped on wild horse creek this evening. After we had ben to camp about 1½ hours Mr. Houston came up and said that Shafer had killed a beef 2 miles below at the camp of Co A no 2 an[d] wanted help to bring it up so 11 or 12 of us went down and brought it up.

**FEBRUARY 24th Sunday.** Another beautiful morning. We are not going to move to day from this camp. This evening as I went up the Creek I found little yellow flower[s] the grass is growing lively.

**FEBRUARY 25th Monday.** About 12 o clock last night I was waked by the yelling of the Indians. I got up and got my gun and found that they wer driving of our horses and mules. They fired 2 guns we returned one shot but we could not stop them. Our animals wer gone. We hapened to stake several horses those they did not get. As soon as practicable I sent Mesrs Badger and Day to camp to get relief. We then commenced fortifying our position by ditching. Day light came and no Indians in sight. I sent out Jacob R. John to see if any body wer camped below. He found no camp but reported that he saw several horses. We started immediately to see if they wer our horses. We found four in one place but could not drive them to camp they being so frightened. 3 men on horses pursued on the trail they found several animals and one mule dead. The[y] also found a rifle and an Indian cap which they [appear] to have lost by being thrown from a horse. Late in the evening 4 men from Company K came to our relief. The Polk County Company is camped 3 miles below this evening.[165]

**FEBRUARY 26th Tuesday.** There was a heavy fall of snow last night. Myself and Mr. Houston started early to the camp of Company B to get them to remain here til we could get the means to remove the provisions from this place. They have camped a half [mile] below this place.[166]

**FEBRUARY 27th Wensday.** A cold frosty morning. Company B sent out men to hunt up cattle they drove in several head. The Linn and Yamhill Companies are camped below this place this evening. Mesrs Badger and Day returned this evening from head quarters. They informed us that 5 wagons wer coming to relieve us and we learned by them that a large number of horses had ben driven of from Camp Cornelius.[167]

**FEBRUARY 28th Thursday.** A cold frosty morning. This morning the wagons came to our camp. We soon had all things in the wagons and with light hearts left this place. We are camped on pinny Creek this evening. This has ben a bright suny day.

**FEBRUARY 29th Friday.** A cold frosty morning. Last night 3 horses and 1 pack mule came to camp. We started early this morning at noon I got leave of Lieutenant Smith[168] to come on to camp. I got to camp about one [hour] before sundown. Things look quit[e] different to what they did when I left there being 3 new [companies] on the ground and [a] fourth one shortly after. They have camped a half mile below this camp. There had ben a liberty pole raised from the top of which our national colors unfolded themselves to the wind. The men employed on the boats have finished three and are now doing nothing for the want of nails.

*Kamayakhen*
*head Chief of the Yakimas*

*Kamiakin, Yakima Chief.*

**MARCH 1, 1856. Saturday.** A frosty morning. Lieutenant Hardin went with a party to hunt nails. About 2 o clock 2 men came to camp from Lieutenant Col Kellys escort they said that the Col would be in camp in half an hour. The Regiment was ordered to parade under arms immediately. After we had formed we had to wait some time before the arival of the Col. When he came up he rode in front of the

Regiment with his hat of and as he past each Company they fired a salut Adjutant Farrar giving the word to fire. Last of all the Howitzer fired after which the Col dismounted and shook hands with all that came his way. The Col lost all but one of his horses on the Umatilla they being drove of by the Indians. They found a fiew old taky [horses] to bring them to camp.

**MARCH 2nd [Sunday].** A beautiful morning. Nothing of importance going on to day. This evening I went with 9 men to dry Creek to waylay Indians if any should pass that way.

**MARCH 3rd Monday.** A warm morning. We saw nor heard any Indians last night. I noticed as I returned to camp this morning several yellow flowers spring seems to be advancing fast. The waggons have started back to the Dalls. There has ben a party of men sent to the Tucannon to meet Lieutenant Wright and Myers who have gone to the Nez Perce country to get horses to remount the men.[169] This evening the second Battalion of the first Regiment elected Mr. Curl ther Junior Major.

**MARCH 4th [Tuesday].** A beautiful warm morning. About noon to day an Indian came to camp being the prisoner that Lieutenant Hannon took down to the valey a short time back. He had a pass from Nathan Olney the Indian Agent at the Dalls. He brought a letter to the Col stating he was sent to Kamiakin the Yacama chief to offer him terms of peace. He wished first to go to the Nez Perce country to see his wife and then he was to go to the camp of Kamiakin if the [Col is] willing but the Col declines employing him as a herald of peace at present. About two o clock Captain Embry of Co E arived in camp. His company paraded and fired a salute ther was two shots fired by the Howitzer. Old Ned Robinson one of the expressmen that caried the express to the Dalls that was sent on the evening of the 8th of December the second day of the Battle [arived in camp].

**MARCH 5th [Wensday].** A pleasant morning. An express of ten men was started to the Dalls this morning to get amunition a pretty time indeed to be sending for amunition.[170] A little change has taken place to relieve the monotony by [the] running of foot races.

**MARCH 6th Thursday.** Last night some of the party that went to the Tucannon got back they came to get provision. They started early this morning back. About ten o clock Liutenant Myers got back to camp from the Nez Perce country. They could not get more than 40 horses. About one o clock 25 recruits for Co D got to camp they wer received with military honors.[171]

**MARCH 7th Friday.** A frosty morning. A[t] eleven o clock one of the Indian prisoners was hung his crime was being a spy. This morning there was a[n] election for Senior Major Captain Conoyer of Company K was elected.[172]

**MARCH 8th Saturday.** About 10 o clock Company E started for the Tushe as the advance guard to the expedition over Snake River. About two o clock I left camp in company with several men and 2 waggons being a part of 50 men detailed to ocupy fort Walla Walla Lieutenant Pillow being in command. We camped 4 miles below Camp Cornelius. Spring is advancing rapidly.[173]

**MARCH 9th Sunday.** A frosty morning. We waited quite late for the Lieutenant when a vote was taken whether we should go on or not. It was the unanimous [opinion] of all hand[s] that we should go on. Shortly after starting we saw Co K on there march at the crossing of Mill Creek.[174] The Liutenant Commisary Fauntleroy and the Indian prisoner came up. We passed Whitmans station and the Battleground[175] We found a cash of potatoes. We camped on dry Creek it does not deserve that name at present for it came very [near] ruining our animals. Grass scarce.

**MARCH 10th Monday.** After some hunting for our animals we left camp crossed the Tushe and camped where the Road crossed the Walla Walla. Gras and wood both scarce.

**MARCH 11th Tuesday.** A frosty morning. We started early crossed the River and the ox teams ascended the hill with difficulty. At the lower crossing while waiting for the wagons those in advance discovered some Indians. After the wagons were across 6 men wer left with the wagons. When the advance got to the fort they saw som[e] 7 or 8 Indians on the oposite side of the River. We found most of the wood work of the fort burned up it having ben burned by the Indians. There is no grass near the fort.

**MARCH 12th Wensday.** A cold cloudy morning. About 10 o clock Captain Wilson arived at this place.[176] They brought but one wagon with them. There is no prospect of any provision being here in less than 8 or 10 days. About noon lieutenant Stillwell left here on his way to Col Cornelius with the amunition packed on mules leaving the wagon at this place.[177] Shortly after he left an expressman arived here from Col Cornelius. He said that the spye had saw about 50 Indians an[d] a vast quantity of stock and that the Regiment would cross 8 miles above the mouth of Snake River.

**MARCH 13th Thursday.** A cold windy morning. I was sent out with the horse guard to day. We crossed the Walla Walla River near the mouth and then drove the stock up the River. The grass [is] very scarce around this place. I noticed to day at one place where the ground was covered with small yellow flowers.

**MARCH 14th Friday** A cold calm morning. We mounted a large iron cannon that we found in the River.[178] This has ben a calm pleasant day. Late in the evening the scouting party sent yesterday came in driving a number of wild horses and colts. They found no cattle.

**MARCH 15th [Saturday].** A cold frosty calm morning. After breakfast I went up the Walla Walla to hunt potatoes about the fields 2 miles above this place but could find none. This has been a calm pleasant day. A little before sundown 2 men got to the fort and reported that they had left Snake River this morning with the waggons and that they would be here to night. They report having seen but about 50 Indians. They had killed 9 Indians and had taken one boy prisoner aged about 6 years he is quite an interesting little chap. They found 3 or 4 hundred head of stock they could [not] mak them cross the River.

**MARCH 16th Sunday.** A cloud[y] windy morning. The prospect is getting quite dreary about something to eat. Captain Wilson went down the River Road where he saw five Indians afoot an[d] the sixth one bringing up a canoe in which they crossed ove[r] with some 25 or 30 men to see if they could find them. They found the canoe but the Indians wer gone. A party of 6 men crossed over this morning and went up the Columbia. They discovered quite a number of horses and they suposed that there was a number of Indians close about but did not see them.

**MARCH 17th [Monday].** A calm pleasant morning. There was sent 2 wagons and 15 men up to Camp Cornelius to bring away such things as had ben left ther. A party of 15 or 20 men went up the Columbia River in three of the boats to see if they could discover any Indians. They saw nothing but a fiew wild horses. This has ben a pleasant day.

**MARCH 18th Tuesday.** About 3 o clock this morning the wind rose very high and has ben blowing as hard as it often blows. This fort is a miserable place for this kind of weather the sand and dirt flying into every thing. We have drawn the last flour in the Commissary department this morning which was a half pound per man. We have had but half rations of flour since the ninth of this month and our beef has ben miserable poor we have no beef at this place but poor milk cows. About 9 o clock this morning 7 men arrived here from Col Cornelius having left the Camp 2 miles below the mouth of the palouse. They report the Regiment destitute of provisions of evry kind. They brought orders for the wagons with the provisions to come on to Snake River as soon as they got here.

**MARCH 19th Wensday.** A cloudy warm morning. We left the fort and moved 3 miles up the Walla Walla River. Shortly after we got our tents pitched we saw 2 men coming on horseback up the Road. They proved to be Captain Cason of the Clackamas Company and Mr. Johnsons the Wagon Master. They camped 12 miles from here last night. It is astonishing how something to eat will improve a man['s] temper for my part evry thing looked gloomy this morning this evening I feel perfectly contented. Ther has ben a light fall of rain to day.

**MARCH 20th Thursday.** About eight o clock last night an express arived from the regimental camp on Snake River they report the Regiment destitute of evry thing to eat but horse meat and that the camp was in an actual state of mutiny. The expressmen had orders to return immediately. They started back about eleven o clock. The camp was waked up at 3 o clock this morning so as to be able to make an early start for Snake River.[179] There was sent up seven wagons drawn by mules an[d] 20 pack mules loaded with provisions for the Regiment. The Clackamas Company has moved 2 miles above this camp. The grass is growing very fast. I noticed to day while on horse guard several litle delicat flowers one in particular it was a cluster of very small flower[s] growing on one stem they wer between a flesh colour and a grey. I have noticed several flowers in this vicinity that would be a va[l]uable adition to the flower garden. This has ben a very windy day mixed with a little rain.

**MARCH 21st Friday.** A windy morning the sky is almost obscured by the clouds. There has ben some fishing done of late the kind of fish caught is specled and Mountain Trout. The escort and wagons that wer sent up to Camp Cornelius got back. They drove in several horses. The wagons brought down the bodies of Liutenant Burrows and Private Crow who wer killed in the Battle of Walla Walla. The citizens of Linn County raised the money by subscription to have there bodies brought home they being citizens of that county.

**MARCH 22nd Saturday.** A cloudy windy morning. The Walla Walla River is rising fast. This rise is caused by the snow melting in the Blue Mountains. There was some difficulty in getting the stock across the River this evening.

**MARCH 23rd Sunday.** A warm morning the River is rising very fast.

**MARCH 24th [Monday].** A warm cloudy morning the River has fallen about 5 inches. About 3 o clock men arived in camp from Snake River. They report a good deal of suffering and sickness in the Regiment they had to live 5 days on horse meat. They say that the Regiment will be here in 7 or 8 days. Upon the reception of the provision[s] they started for priests rapids.[180] They took a boat and wagon along with them. There horses are giving out fast. Ther was but 2 wagons out of 7 brought back to this camp.

**MARCH 25th Tuesday.** A warm cloudy morning. The teamsters are geting there wagons across the River and loading them to return to the Dalls. After dark this evening an express was sent to fort Henrietta.

**MARCH 26th Wensday.** A clear warm morning. The wagons started for the Dalls. They have an escort of 25 men. 2 of the boats are sent up to the Mouth of Snake River they will be escorted up by the Clackamas Company. This evening 9 head of cattle wer [driven] into camp by 4 men of the Clackamas Company.

**MARCH 27th Thursday.** During the night the cattle drove up yesterday evening got out of the karaal and left this part of the earth. 3 men went in pursuit but could not overtake them. I have ben out to day on horse guard and I find vegitation advancing rapidly. I have never seen grass grow as fast as it does here at this season of the year. The Walla Walla River is falling fast. There has ben 50 head of cattle drove here this evening by a detachment of Clackamas Company. They found them on the Umatilla. That part of the country seems to have an unlimited suply of cattle for evry party there gets cattle if they but have perseverance. The fact is the Indians have ben driving there stock into that part of the country.

92

*Middle Blockhouse, Cascades of the Columbia.*   Special Collections
University of Washington Libraries

**MARCH 28th Friday.** A pleasant morning. This day has ben quite warm. This evening Mr. Riggs arived here from Henrietta acompanied by 2 men. They have heard nothing of the pack train which should have ben here on the 27th. After sundown the wind rose acompanied by a little rain.

**MARCH 29th [Sunday].** A cloudy warm morning a light fall of rain to day. About 12 o clock to day Lieutenant Caldwell arived in camp.[181] He left the Regiment yesterday. He reports the Regiment in a suffering condition almost destitute of provisions and there horses failing fast. They have found but one cow since they left the palouse River and consequently they have used horse meat all the time. They have seen but fiew Indians. The Regiment will cross the Columbia at the mouth of the Yacama River. The 2 mule teams that took the boats up to the mouth of Snake River came back to get what provision was here. They loaded and returned. Ther was a small shower this afternoon

93

we heard one clap of thunder. Another express for the Dalls this evening.

**MARCH 31st Monday.** About one o clock an express arived here from the Dalls on his way to the Col. They report the Indians killing the inhabitants and burning the houses about the Cascades. The Regulars we[re] ordered back to that place. They wer at 5 mile creek this side of the Dalls. They report 40 pack animals and 4 wagons at John Days River yesterday. We received the information this evening that the Regiment had determined to return to the Dalls part of the Regiment will go down on this side of the Columbia and a part on the other side. The Clackamas Company has returned from the mouth of Snake River to this place.

**APRIL 1, 1856. Tuesday** A cloudy morning a fiew drops of rain fell today. Company A no 2 came down to this place to day.[182].

**APRIL 2nd Wensday.** There was wind and rain last night. A very windy morning. Crossed over to the south side of the Walla Walla River and camped a little below our old camp. The grass is fine. Company K has come down from Snake River. This has ben a windy and cloudy day.

**APRIL 3rd Thursday.** A cloudy morning this has ben a warm cloudy day. I have ben drying beef to day.

**APRIL 4th Friday.** A rainy morning. Our beef cattl got away last night. About 10 o clock myself and 6 others started in pursuit. We went 7 miles up the Walla Walla then we turned up a hollow went up 5 miles and found the cattle. The grass is growing fine. I noticed several beautiful flowering plants. That portion of the Command on the other sid[e] of the Columbia River camped opposite the fort last night. They are destitute of provision the want of suitable food is likely to be a serious affair with some persons. There are several persons sick at present.

**APRIL 5th Saturday.** A cloudy morning. We packed up early and came down to the Columbia River[183] We crossed over in a skiff. We swam our horses over by the side of the skiff. We found our company all in good health. They have had a hard time of it. The pack train got up last night so we have bread once more. Our beef cattle got away last night again. This has ben a cloudy day.

*Site of Middle Cascades Blockhouse, 1867.*

**APRIL 6th Sunday.** Raining this morning. We traveled over a broken country [covered] partly with bunch grass and part with sage the soil is sandy and rocky. Traveled 30 miles and camped on the Yacama River. Grass not plenty wood scarce and poor in quality. Several horses gave [out] to day.

**APRIL 7th Monday.** A clear morning. We voted on the question of a convention or no convention to draft a constitution preparitory to Oregon becoming a state. There was a considerable majority against a convention. Company A all went against the convention. We saw on the mountains a number of cattle. We traveled up the Yacama River the country near the River is covered with sage the ground is rocky the mountain[s] on our left are covered with bunch grass. Traveled 10 miles and camped on the River. A pretty good place to camp grass handy and wood sufficient for our purposes. There is nothing but brush along the bank of this river and even that is scarc. The snow is in sight of the Cascade Mountains. Captain Hembree has brought in part of a beef he killed.

**APRIL 8th Tuesday.** A frosty morning. We traveled up the River the country is allmost barren. We crossed cow trail the cattle in this part of the country are as wild as Buffalo. There is more sign of timber on the River than below. We traveled 20 miles the country arond camp is covered with sage and prickly pears ther [is] allmost no grass at this place.

**APRIL 9th [Wensday].** A cloudy morning. Traveled up the River several [miles] passed some fertile bottom land covered with a luxuriant growth of coarse grass. We passed an Indian graveyard. The general features of the country is mountainous barren rocky sandy and covered with sage and prickly pears. Traveled 14 miles and camped on the Simcoe a large Creek a tributary of the Yacama River its banks are lined with a small growth of timber. There is tolerable fair grass at this camp. The Yacama River has no tributary for 50 miles from its mouth. It takes its rise in the Cascade Range of Mountains an[d] runs East and fall[s] into the Columbia River some 10 miles above the mouth of Snake River. This evening a dust was noticed above here Col Cornelius and several others went up to see if any Indians wer about. They saw 2 Indians.

**APRIL 10th Thursday.** Early this morning Captain Wilson Hembree and Wilber with 6 other men started out to reconnoiter crossed over to the right of the Creek and when they had got near the sumit of the hills the Indians charged on them from 3 sides. Captain Hembree was killed at the first fire the balance escaped by dashing down a bluff. We saw the Indians in camp before they saw them. Several men started immediately to there relief on foot. The diferent companies we[re] ordered to arms immediately. Some got there horses and went in pursuit of the Indians. As they invariably fled wenever attacted it was but a short time till the Indians wer out of sight. They returned to camp and reported that they would oppose our passing throug a canyon some 4 miles above. We got ready to start but there wer 3 men of Co B and C that had gone back to our camp of the night before last to hunt horses that wer lost.[184] It would not do to leave them. 24 men wer detailed to go back an[d] see what had become of them. They wer not gone long till they met one of them with several horses but he did not know where the others wer. Part of the detachment came back with him the others went on till they could see the camp. They saw nothing of the missing men and returned leaving 2 notices of our difficulty. The Col determined not to leave till morning so we unpacked and Major Connoyer went out to see if he could find the

Indians. Shortly after leaving the Indians made there appearence at the same place that they did in the morning. They fled on the approach of the men. The 2 missing men came in between 4 and 5 o clock. They wer chased 5 miles by the Indians. They thought they killed one. Major Conoyer and party returned after dark. They had a skirmish fight with the Indians. They killed one Indian and scalped him. They thought they wounded 2 or 3 more. They estimated the number of Indians at from 150 to 200 and upward.

**APRIL 11th Friday.** There was a heavy fall of rain last night. The guard fired several false alarms last night they shot one horse in the neck. At half past 9 o clock we left camp. Company E brought the body of Captain Hembree along with them. They intend to take it to the Dalls and send it to his family. We traveled up the Creek a short distance we then traveled over the hills for several miles we then returned to the Creek an[d] traveled the remainder of the day. Traveled 18 miles to day. Fine grass.

**APRIL 12th Saturday.** A frosty morning. A little after sunup some Indians wer discovered on the right hand bluff opposite the camp. They made no attempt to atact us but stood watching us till we left. We had some fear that they would atact us on our march so evry precaution was taken to prevent a surprise that the nature of the country would admit of for it is very rough and mountainous. Our route lay up the creek we passed throug some very narrow defiles. About noon to day the advance guard met 2 Indians they attempted to get away but wer shot and scalped. They had one gunn. They wer supposed to be Clickatat Indians. The grass is growing fine on the Simcoe Mountains. We crossed the summit of [the] Mountains and camped on a branch of the Clickatat. Our camp is in the pine timber. The grass is fine. Our road lay through narrow defiles in thickets of brush it would not have taken many resolut men to have stoped our march. Traveled 20 miles.[185]

**APRIL 13th Sunday.** A frosty morning. Company E started early so as to reach the Dalls to day. The object is to forward Captain Hembree['s] body on home as soon as practicable. We traveled 6 miles down the creek and camped in the open prarie. The pack train with a detachment went on to the Dalls to bring out provision. The grass is fine through this part of the country.

**APRIL 14th Monday.** A cold windy morning. We eat up all the flour for breakfast. We have had nothing since last Tuesday evening but

97

flour and coffee to eat. This has ben a windy day. After dark the pack train got back from the Dalls with provisions.

**APRIL 15th Tuesday.** A frosty morning this has ben disagreeable day with an occasional light shower of rain. Our horses are improving in spirit and flesh fast.

**APRIL 16th Wensday.** A cloudy morning. A part of the pack train returns to the Dalls to day for provisions. Among the vegitables growing about camp is the wild onion or garlick cammuse and another bulbous rooted plant having a top like a carrot. Late this evening there was driven to this camp a lot of beef cattle they wer brought from the Dalls.

**APRIL 17th Thursday.** A warm cloudy morning. At 9 o clock the horses wer driven in and we sadled up and started for the Dalls. The country over which [we traveled] was covered with bunch grass. We passed over some very fertile spots. I have seen some very beautiful specimens of flowers to day. We camped 4 miles from the Dalls on a smal branch. Grass is abundant wood scarce. There has ben 5 beeves killed this evening.

**APRIL 18th Friday.** A warm pleasant morning. There are a great many crickets and grasshopers about this place. We can form no idea of what we are going to do next. Rumor has it that we are goin home shortly and again that we are to return to the Yackama Country.[186] This has ben a very warm day.

**APRIL 19th Saturday.** A cloudy windy morning. I started to the Dalls this morning. When I got to the River I found quite a number of persons waiting to get over but there was no boat to ferry us over so I returned to camp. This has ben a disagreeable windy day.

**APRIL 20th Sunday.** A clear morning with a light breeze. About 8 o clock Captain Ankeny came up from the Dalls and said that it was reported in camp that there was a large body of Indians at the mouth of the Clickatat. The Captain took 50 men with him an[d] went out down to see. When they got down they found no Indians and but little sign of any. They got back befor sundown. This has ben a fine day. There came into camp 5 Indians. They had a White flag. They had ben sent out by Major Haller to the Yacama Country. There was 8 men detached to escort them to the River.

**APRIL 21st Monday.** A cloudy morning. I went down to the Dalls early this morning. I found Captain Wilson at the hospital his lungs are seriously affected. It is rumored that we will have to return to the Walla Walla Country. Col Cornelius is going to see the governor in person and advise him as to the best course to be pursued. Captain Wilson has wrote a letter to the governor asking the discharge of Company A. Ther has ben a light fall of rain to day.

**APRIL 22nd Tuesday.** A cold clear morning. Nothing of importance going on to day. This has ben a cool day throughout.

**APRIL 23rd Wensday.** A cloudy morning about 9 o clock there fell a shower of rain. Liutenant Pillow drew a quantity of clothing from the Quarter Master department. I got a pair of shoes 2 pair of socks the boys are dressing quite fine for camp life. We heard this morning the whistle of the steamer Mary. She came up yesterday evening from the Cascades and reported 2 Companies of United States troops coming up for which she was to return immediately to the Cascades. We have some reason to believe that we will be discharged shortly. This has ben a disagreeable day.

**APRIL 24th Thursday.** A frosty morning. It rained freely in the fore part of the night. While raining here it snowed on the mountains. Several men of our company went several miles up the Columbia to an old Indian village to hunt cashes. They found several cashes of lumber which was used by the Indians in making there huts in the fishing season. They also found some cooking utensil[s] such as buckets pots and mortars. This has ben a windy day.

**APRIL 25th Friday.** A cool morning. I went to the Dalls for to see Mr. Fisher. I found him. He said that my carpet sack was coming down in the wagons I left it with him at Walla Walla. Ther is some prospect of our geting discharged shortly a thing that we all ardently hope will soon come. Company B took one of there men on a litter to the Dalls. He was taken violently sick last night and the Doctor was sent for. It is reported that the Regulars will cross the River on Monday next. Liutenant Hardin has come back to the Company after an absence of 3 weeks or more.

**April 26th Saturday.** A pleasant morning. About eight o clock we wer called together to hear a speech from Commisary general McCarver. This gentleman came to our camp yesterday he said that governor

*S.S. Wasco at The Dalles.*

Curry has requested him to come and see us. He advised us to wait patiently until the Col returned and he thought that we would get discharged. He furthermore said that we had gone through a campaign umparallelled in history for its hardship and privations. He said that he wanted an investigation of his official character an[d] if he wer to blame for our not being suplyed he was willing to bair the blame. He said that he had the books to show that he had purchased full rations for the Regiment untill the first of June. He could not say who was to blame for it not being forwarded to us but ther wa[s] [a] screw loose somewher.

**APRIL 27th [Sunday].** A cloudy morning. We have nothing to relieve the monotony of camp life. There has ben a light sprinkle of rain.

**APRIL 28th Monday.** About seven o clock this morning a party of Indians made a dash at our horses and run them of. They wer about a half a mile from camp guarded by 6 or 7 men. We gathered our gunns ran out to the top of the hill the Indians wer beyond our reach. There was a fiew horses staked about camp these we sadled immediately and started in pursuit. The Indians had got the start so that they could not overtake them. This stamped has striped us of our horses. About 9 o clock Major Connoyer and Doctor Smith and Ballard arived in camp from the Dalls. The Major ordered a parade of the Battalion. He said that he felt very bad about the horses being gone and said that he felt like trying to recover the [horses] an[d] get the Indians hair. A company of Dragoons under the command of Captain Davidson came up to see if [we] needed any assistence. They had the finest lot of horses I have seen for a greate while. Liutenant Hardin has gone over

100

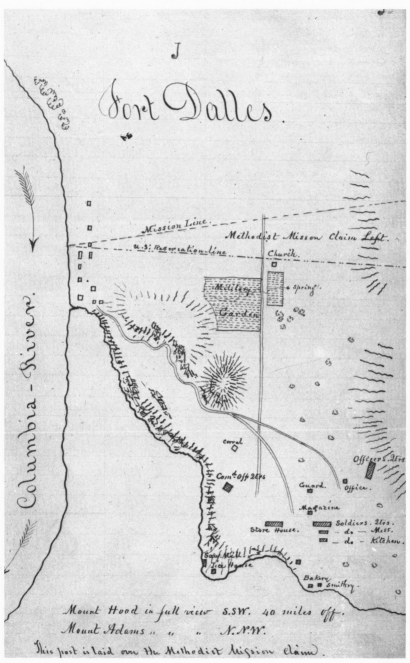

Fort Dalles.

the River to get horses to remount Company A. The object is to remount the Battalion and pursue the Indians.

**APRIL 29th Tuesday.** A pleasant morning. I went to the Dalls early. I found the Regulars encamped on this side of the River. The Steamer Mary was ferrying over the pack animals. These troops are going to the Yackama Country. They intend taking provision sufficient to last them 3 months. There is 5 companies of them there is about 80 of them mounted. They have 3 Mountain Howitzers. They have traveled about 6 miles from the landing. When I got into the Dalls I found Liutenant Pillow and Myers engaged in getting the horses shod for our contemplated pursuit of the Indians. I borrowed one dollar of Mr. Fritze to buy pens Ink and a blank Book. I also got some cough medicine of the Surgeon. I returned to camp when I got back I was very sick. This has ben quite a pleasant day.

**APRIL 30th Wensday.** A warm morning. Early this morning companies B and C of the new Battalion [packed up] and went down to the Dalls. This was an act of there own as no officer ordered them to do so. About 10 o clock the Steamer Wasco arived from the Cascades bringing Col Cornelius and Captains Wilson and Ankeny. We all removed to the Dalls this evening in order to start to Portland to morrow. This news was received with great pleasure by all the men. We all have got sick and tired of Military service. We long to greete the loved ones at home. A greate many of us have ben out well on to 7 months and have indured a great deall of hardship and suffering owing to the severity of the weather and the want of provision.

**MAY 1, 1856. Thursday.** A warm morning. Company A and D went on board of the Steamer Wasco. The wind had got quit[e] high befor we started. We came down 4 miles and had to land on account of Drunk men and the roughness of the River. The bluffs of the River ar[e] composed of Basaltick Rock and are extremely broken.

**MAY 2nd Friday.** We started early this morning the wind was quit[e] high the River got quit[e] rough before we got to the Cascades. There are several houses along the River but unocupied at present. They have ben abandoned since the Masacree at the Cascades. The Mountains as we approach the Cascades are covered with pine timber. We landed about noon at the Cascades. We waited for the return of the wagons. We then started for the lower landing. There is a wagon road around the falls its about 2 miles long at this point. The freight is shiped in bateaux to the foot of the rapids.

102

**MAY 3rd Saturday.** We tak[e] the Steamer Fashion and arived at Portland about 2 o clock. This morning I had one of the worst chills I ever had in my life and I have not often ben as sick and to add to my misery there was no place about the Boat that I could lay down the Boat was crowded from stem to stern. Here I am at home again after an absense of 203 days having left on the 13th of October last. I found Father Mother Brothers and Sisters all anxious to minister to my wants. I cannot conceive why it is that so many youths aband[o]n ther Fathers house to wander in distant lands among strangers who feel no other interest in him but a selfish interest. What can be more consoling in affliction than a Fathers attention and Mothers care. We are apt to think light of these things while we enjoy good health but let affliction come and then if among strangers we realize the fact that a Mothers care cannot be suplyed by others.

# Abbreviations

CaBViP   Provincial Archives, Victoria, B.C.

CSmH   Henry E. Huntington Library and Art Gallery, San Marino, California.

CtY   Yale University Library, New Haven, Connecticut.

CUB   Bancroft Library, University of California, Berkeley, California.

HBC   Hudson's Bay Company, Beaver House, Great Trinity Lane, London, England.

LC   Manuscript Division, Library of Congress, Washington, D.C.

MD   Maryland Historical Society, Baltimore, Maryland.

NA   National Archives, Washington, D.C.

Record Group 75: Records of the Office of Indian Affairs, Treaty Talks and Treaties.

Record Group 94: Office of the Adjutant General, Letters Received.

Record Group 123: U.S. Court of Claims.

Record Group 393: Records of the United States Army Commands.

OHQ   *Oregon Historical Quarterly.*

OHS   Oregon Historical Society, Portland, Oregon.

OrA   State of Oregon, Archives Division, State Library Building, Salem, Oregon.

PNQ   *Pacific Northwest Quarterly.*

UofO   University of Oregon Library, Eugene, Oregon.

| | |
|---|---|
| UofW | Special Collections: University of Washington Library, Seattle, Washington. |
| Wa | Washington State Library, Olympia, Washington. |
| WaSp | Northwest History Collection, Spokane Public Library, Spokane, Washington. |
| WHQ | *Washington Historical Quarterly.* |
| WHS | Washington State Historical Society, Tacoma, Washington. |

# Notes

1. L.V. McWhorter, "The Bolon Tragedy as Narrated by Sul-lil: Sole Survivor and Eye-Witness." Typescript. *WHS*. This account was published as *Tragedy of the Wahk-Shun. Prelude to the Yakima Indian War, 1855-1856. Eye-Witness Account of the Killing of Indian Agent Major Andrew J. Bolon, Together with Story of Locating the Place of his Death, Regional Indian Legends, and Definition of "Yakima,"* Yakima, Wa., The Author, 1937.
2. G.O. Haller, "The Indian War of 1855-56." Typescript. *UofW*.
3. *Weekly Oregonian* (Portland), Sept. 29, 1855, p. 2.
4. George Gibbs to George McClellan, Olympia, W.T., March 4, 1854. *LC*. This report was published in *Reports of Explorations and Surveys, to Ascertain the Most Practicable and Economical Route for a Railroad from the Mississippi River to the Pacific Ocean*, I: 402-34.
5. Hubert H. Bancroft, *History of Oregon*, II: 261.
6. C.F. Coan, "Federal Indian Relations of the Pacific Northwest," *OHQ*, XXII (1921), 54ff.
7. Charles J. Kappler, ed., *Indian Affairs: Laws and Treaties*, II: 661, 669, 674, 682.
8. *Ibid.*, II: 661, 665.
9. Doty to Stevens, Walla Walla Valley, Treaty Grounds, Camp Stevens, May 22, 1855. Ms. *NA: RG 75*.
   "Journal of Operations of Governor Isaac Ingalls Stevens, Superintendent of Indian Affairs and Commissioner, treating with the Indian Tribes East of the Cascade Mountains, in Washington Territory, and the Blackfeet and Neighboring Tribes, near the Great Falls of Missourie, in the year 1855;

including therein details of the celebrated Indian Council at Walla Walla, and of the Blackfoot Council at Fort Benton, and the Commencement of the Indian Wars, 1855-8." *NA: RG* 75; Typescript, p. 12, 15, 17. *WaSp.*

10. "Official Proceedings of the council held at the council ground in the Walla Walla Valley, with the Yakima nation of Indians . . . May 28, 1855-June 9, 1855," *NA:RG* 75; printed in *34th Cong. 1 Sess. Sen. Ex. Doc. No. 30.*

11. Richard H. Lansdale, "Diary" June 8, 1855. Ms. *CtY.*

12. "Official Proceedings of the council held at the council ground in the Walla Walla Valley, etc." Ms. *NA: RG* 75.

13. Kappler, *op. cit.* II: 694, 698.

14. Quoted by Plympton Kelly, Dec. 20, 1855. This assurance was not reflected in the privately expressed apprehensions a few days before the treaty was signed and, even more significantly, on the very day Kamiakin affixed his mark to the document, June 9, 1855. Doty, the council secretary, noted on May 26, 1855, that "reports are in circulation that Pee-Opee-Mox-a-Mox, the Cayuse and Yakimas have combined and are determined to make no Treaty etc., and the settlers fear the Indians will commit acts of hostility in case they are urged to treat." The actual signing of the agreement two weeks later was muted by Kamiakin's parting reminder that "when the treaty had been approved by the President, and the Indians moved out of their reservation, then he would accept his share of the goods." "Journal of Operations of Governor Isaac Ingalls Stevens, etc.," *NA: RG* 75; Typescript, p. 16, 21, *WaSp.*

15. *Weekly Oregonian* June 23, 1855, p. 2.

16. *ibid.*, June 30, 1855, p. 2; July 7, 1855, p. 2.

17. *ibid.*, July 14, 1855, p. 2; July 21, 1855, p. 2.

18. *ibid.*, Sept. 1, 1855, p. 2; Sept. 22, 1855, p. 2; Sept. 29, 1855, p. 2.

19. *ibid.*, July 28, 1855, p. 2; *Oregon Statesman*, Sept. 1, 1855, p. 2; John T. Kern, "Diary," Sept. 22, 1855, Ms. No. 1095, *OHS.*

20. L.V. McWhorter, "The Bolon Tragedy as Narrated by Sul-lil: Sole Survivor and Eye-Witness," Typescript, *WHS.*

21. The introductory essay supplies a brief narrative backdrop for a clearer understanding of the action described in Plympton Kelly's diary. This essay, although based on much new research, is not a comprehensive history of the Yakima War, 1855-1856, much less is it a revealing study of Indian hostilities in mid-nineteenth century Oregon.

22. *Weekly Oregonian*, Sept. 29, 1855, p. 2; M. M. McCarver to George Curry, [Salem], Oct. 2, 1855. Ms. *OrA*; Dugald Mactavish to W. G. Smith, Vancouver, Oct. 10, 1855. Ms. Quoted by permission of the Hudson's Bay Company, hereafter cited as *HBC*.

23. G. O. Haller, "The Indian War of 1855-56." Typescript. Quoted by permission of the University of Washington Library: hereafter cited as *UofW*.

24. G. O. Haller, "Journal of a scout in the Yakima country," Oct. 6, 1855. Ms. *UofW*.

25. Haller, "The Indian War of 1855-56." Typescript. *UofW*. Conditions were never too critical for making money. The steamship *Wasco* charged $100 for carrying the "special express with despatches to Hd Qrs Col[umbia] River & Puget Sound District" on October 8th; there was a $50 ferrying charge the next day for transporting Lt. Day's Co L, 3d Artillery, relief column across the Columbia, and a $75 fee for "Ferrying Bvt. Maj. Haller's command of Co L 3d Arty & Cos I & K 4th Infty returning from the Expedition against the Yakimas" on Oct. 10, 1855. "Report of Persons and Articles employed and hired at Fort Dalles, O.T. during the Month of October 1855." "Ms. *NA: RG* 92.

26. J. P. Keller to Charles Foster*, Teekalet, W.T., Nov. 1, 1855; Keller to Foster, Teekalet, W.T., Nov. 11, 1855. Ms. *CtY*.

27. Order No. 17, Fort Vancouver, Oct. 9, 1855. Ms. *NA: RG* 393.

28. G. Rains to Gov. George Curry, Fort Vancouver, Oct. 9, 1855. Ms. *NA: RG* 393.

29. Andrew J. Cain to Charles Mason, Cascades, Oct. 9, 1855. Ms. *Wa*.

30. Rains to Adjt. Genl. Samuel Cooper, Fort Vancouver, Dec. 1, 1855. Ms. *NA: RG* 94.

31. Rains to Mason, Yakima Camp No. 4, W.T., Nov. 4, 1855. Ms. *Wa*.; Rains to Curry, Yakima Camp No. 4, W.T., Nov. 4, 1855. Ms. *OrA*.

32. *Weekly Oregonian*, Oct. 13, 1855, p. 2; *Correspondence and Official Proceedings Relating to the Expeditions Against the Indians* (Salem, Asahel Bush, Territorial Printer, 1855) 6.

33. Curry to James Nesmith, Dalles, Nov. 3, 1855, in *ibid.*, p. 33; Wasco to the editor, Dalles, O.T., Nov. 1, 1855, in *Weekly Oregonian*, Nov. 10, 1855, p. 2; Jon to Editor Thomas J. Dryer, Dalles, O.T., Oct. 30, 1855, in *Weekly Oregonian*, Nov. 3, 1855, p. 2; M. P. Deady to A. Bush, Fairoaks, Douglas Co., Ore., Jan.

21, 1856, and J. W. Drew to Bush, Deer Creek, O.T., Nov. 16, 1855. Ms. *UofO*; V. W. Schaeffer to his mother, Portland, O.T., May 11, 1856, Ms. No. 1086, *OHS*; M. M. McCarver to the editor, May 16, 1856, in (Portland) *Oregon Weekly Times*, May 24, 1856, p. 2.

34. *Weekly Oregonian*, Oct. 20, 1855, p. 1.

35. A. J. Price, "A Journal of Col. Nesmith's Expedition," in *ibid.*, Nov. 24, 1855, p. 2. No attempt has been made in this narrative essay or the editorial notes to follow the campaign in southern Oregon. The Second Regiment, Oregon Mounted Volunteers, had more men in the field in the spring and summer, 1856, fighting the Rogue River Indians and neighboring tribes, than the First Regiment did against the Yakimas. The problems of transport, purchase, and supply were almost as great as they were in the north. This war in the south affected progress against the northern tribes because it added immensely to the overall strain on the resources of the territory. I have chosen to restrict myself to a mere mention of this parallel struggle because it is a distinct story separate from the events described by Plympton J. Kelly in his diary.

36. Curry to N. A. Cornoyer, Portland, Oct. 24, 1855, in *Correspondence and Official Proceedings*, 24.

37. *Weekly Oregonian,* Oct. 20, 1855; p. 2; A. H. Sale, "Indian War Recollections," *Oregon Native Son*, I (1899-1900), 333; Edmond S. Meany, ed., "Waman C. Hembree Yakima Indian War Diary," *WHQ*, XVI (1925), 274-75; Curry to A. F. Hedges, Portland, Oct. 13, 1855, in *Correspondence and Official Proceedings*, 9; Nesmith to Curry, Cascades, W.T., Oct. 18, 1855, in *ibid.*, 16; Curry to Nesmith, Portland, Oct. 21, 1855, in *ibid.*, 18; "Captain Charles Bennett," *Ladd & Bush Quarterly*, II (1914), 3; A. V. Wilson to Curry, Lower Cascades, Oct. 15, 1855. Ms. No. 923 *OrA*; (Portland) *Oregon Weekly Times*, Oct. 27, 1855, p. 2; C. B. Pillow to T. J. Dryer, Oct. 24, 1855, in *Weekly Oregonian*, Nov. 10, 1855, p. 2.

38. Nesmith to Curry, Cascades, W.T., Oct. 18, 1855, in *Correspondence and Official Proceedings*, 16.

39. Curry to Nesmith, Portland, Oct. 21, 1855, *ibid.*, 18; Nesmith to Curry, Fort Dalles, O.T., Oct. 22, 1855, in *ibid.*, 19; Curry to Nesmith, Portland, Oct. 23, 1855, in *ibid.*, 20.

40. *Weekly Oregonian*, Oct. 20, 1855, p. 1; Curry to Wilson, Portland, O.T., Oct. 13, 1855, in *Correspondence and Official Proceedings*, 7; Curry to Wilson, Portland, O.T., Oct. 16, 1855, in *ibid.*,

12. The steamer *James R. Flint* was 60 feet long, with a 12 foot beam, and five foot draft. She had been built in 1851 by D. F. Bradford, P. E. Bradford, J. O. Vanbergen, and James R. Flint of San Francisco. She was on the Dalles-Cascade run until Jan. 1, 1852, when the owners moved her to the Portland-Cascades route until she sank near Cape Horn on the Columbia River. She was raised, lengthened, and with the engine from the old *Columbia* installed, renamed *Fashion.*

41. C. B. Pillow to T. J. Dryer, Dalles, O.T., Oct. 24, 1855, in *Weekly Oregonian*, Nov. 10, 1855, p. 2; (Portland) *Oregon Weekly Times*, Oct. 27, 1855, p. 2. Daniel F. Bradford and Putnam E. Bradford had built the 80 foot long sidewheeler, *Mary*, at the Cascades in 1854; and used her on the run to The Dalles until she was dismantled in 1862.

42. Some of the men built stone houses as shelters for themselves at Three Mile Creek: the first of these being named Fort Wilson in honor of their company commander. Other men made tents with their blankets, preferring a shelter from the wind more than a cover for themselves. Pillow to Dryer, The Dalles, O.T., Oct. 24, 1855 in *Weekly Oregonian*, Nov. 10, 1855, p. 2.

43. The *Gazelle* was launched at Canemah in 1854. She was 120 feet long, with a 20 foot beam, and a six foot draft. Shortly after being put in operation, her boilers exploded at the dock in Canemah killing 20 and injuring 11 people, April 8, 1854. The engineless hull was pressed into service during the Yakima War as a barge towed by one of the other steamboats. The 108 foot *Multnomah* was built at Oregon City in 1851, used on the upper Willamette River for a year, when she was placed on the Oregon City-Portland run. Eventually she was purchased by the Oregon Steam Navigation Co., 1863, and dismantled the following year.

44. The ten initial companies comprising the First Regiment, Oregon Mounted Volunteers, that campaigned against the northern tribes were:

Co. A, Multnomah County, mustered Oct. 15, 1855, 97 rank and file, Capt. A. V. Wilson, 1st Lt. B. M. Harding, 2nd Lt., C. B. Pillow.

Co. B, Wasco County, mustered Oct. 18, 1855, 65 rank and file, Capt. O. Humason, 1st Lt. John T. Jeffries, 2nd Lt. James McAuliff.

Co. C, Clackamas County, mustered Oct. 16, 1855, 93 rank and file, Capt. James K. Kelly (was elected Lt. Colonel, First

Regiment, Oct. 30, 1855), Capt. Samuel Stafford* (elected Nov. 4, 1855), 1st Lt. D. B. Hannah, 2nd Lt. J. A. Pownall*, 2nd Lt. Charles Cutting* (elected Nov. 4, 1855).

Co. D, Washington County, mustered Oct. 17, 1855, 100 rank and file, Capt. Thomas R. Cornelius (elected Colonel, First Regiment, Dec. 21, 1855), 1st Lt. Hiram Wilber, 2nd Lt. W. H. H. Myers, 2nd Lt. John H. Smith* (elected Dec. 30, 1855).

Co. E, Yamhill County, mustered Oct. 17, 1855, 99 rank and file, Capt. A. J. Hembree, 1st Lt. John P. Hibler, 2nd Lt. Wm. H. Wright.*

Co. F, Marion County, mustered Oct. 19, 1855, 81 rank and file, Capt. Charles Bennett (killed Dec. 7, 1855), 1st Lt. A. M. Fellows (elected captain following Bennett's death, Dec. 1855), 2nd Lt. A. Shephard* (elected 1st Lt., Dec. 1855), 2nd Lt. Richard A. Barker* (elected Dec. 1855).

Co. G, Polk County, mustered Oct. 19, 1855, 104 rank and file, Capt. Ambrose N. Armstrong* (elected Major, First Regiment, Oct. 30, 1855: resigned this office Dec. 27, 1855), Capt. Benjamin Hayden (elected Nov. 2, 1855), 1st Lt. Ira S. Townsend,* 2nd Lt. Francis M. P. Goff,* 2nd Lt. David Casper.

Co. H, Linn County, mustered Oct. 20, 1855, 74 rank and file, Capt. Davis Layton, 1st Lt. A. Hanan, 2nd Lt. John M. Burrows.*

Co. I, Benton County, mustered Oct. 20, 1855, 71 rank and file, Capt. Lyman B. Munson, 1st Lt. Smith Suard,* 2nd Lt. Charles B. Hand.*

Co. K, Marion County, mustered Oct. 31, 1855, 30 rank and file, Capt. Narcisse A. Cornoyer, 1st Lt. Antoine Rivais, 2nd Lt. Thomas J. Small.

The expiration of enlistment terms and resignations from various Volunteer companies necessitated the formation of five Recruiting companies to bring the regiment back to operational strength; these were:

Co. A, Capt. E. J. Harding, Jan. 25-May 9, 1856.

Co. B, Capt. Benjamin F. Burch, Jan. 25-May 15, 1856.

Co. C, Capt. A. P. Ankeny, Jan. 29-May 15, 1856.

Co. D, Capt. John H. Settle, Feb. 1-May 26, 1856.

Co. E, Capt. Wm. A. Cason, Feb. 25-June 10, 1856.

"Muster Rolls, First Regiment, Oregon Mounted Volunteers." Ms.; "Muster Rolls, Recruiting Battalions, First Regiment, Oregon Mounted Volunteers." Ms. OrA.

45. Nesmith to Curry, Fort Dalles, O.T., Oct. 22, 1855, in *Correspondence and Official Proceedings*, 19.

46. Jon to T. J. Dryer, Dalles, O.T., Oct. 30, 1855, in *Weekly Oregonian*, Nov. 3, 1855, p. 2.

47. Curry to Nesmith, Dalles, O.T., Nov. 1, 1855, in *Correspondence and Official Proceedings*, 31; A. J. Price, "A Journal of Col. Nesmith's Expedition," from *Weekly Oregonian*, Nov. 24, 1855, p. 2; Wasco to editor, Dalles, O.T., Nov. 1, 1855, in *Weekly Oregonian*, Nov. 10, 1855, p. 2; Curry to Nesmith, Dalles, O.T., Nov. 3, 1855, in *Correspondence and Official Proceedings*, 33; *Weekly Oregonian*, Oct. 27, 1855, p. 2. The steamer *Wasco* was built at the Cascades in 1855 and operated on the Columbia River until 1861.

48. Nesmith to Curry, Dalles, O.T., Nov. 19, 1855, *OHS:* Rains to Cooper, Fort Vancouver, Dec. 1, 1855, Ms. *NA: RG* 94; Meany, ed., "Waman C. Hembree Yakima Indian War Diary," *WHQ*, XVI (1925), 276; Haller, "Memorandum connected with a Scout into the Yakima Country, under Major Rains, 4th Infy," Ms. *UofW*; Rains to Mason, Camp Yakima No. 4, W.T., Nov. 4, 1855, *Wa.*; Rains to Curry, Camp Yakima No. 4, W.T., Nov. 4, 1855, *OrA.* Waman Hembree, "Diary," Nov. 7, 1855, Typescript. *WHS.*

49. Nesmith to Curry, Dalles of the Columbia, Nov. 19, 1855, in *Weekly Oregonian*, Dec. 1, 1855, p. 2; A. H. Sale, "Indian War Recollections," *Oregon Native Son*, I (1899), 334; Haller, "Memorandum connected with a Scout," Nov. 8, 1855. Ms. *UofW*; Haller, "Kamiarkin in History," Ms. *CUB*.

50. *Person Memoirs of P. H. Sheridan, General United States Army* (2 vols., New York, Charles Webster & Company, 1888), I: 60.

51. Nesmith to Curry, Dalles of the Columbia, Nov. 19, 1855, in *Weekly Oregonian*, Dec. 1, 1855, p. 2.

52. Haller, "Kamiarkin in History," Ms. *CUB*: Maloney to Mason, Camp Connell, Nov. 6, 1855, *Wa.*; Nesmith to Curry, Dalles of the Columbia, Nov. 19, 1855, *Weekly Oregonian*, Dec. 1, 1855, p. 2. St. Joseph's Mission was on Ahtanum Creek about two miles east of Nesmith's camp. Catholic missionary work among the Yakimas was started by Pascal Ricard, Charles Pandosy, and Casimir Chirouse, all members of the Oblates of Mary Immaculate, in October 1847. The Whitman Massacre, Nov. 27, 1847, was a grisly outburst of the festering native resentment that failed to cow the newly-arrived priests. Exactly ten years after the mission was looted and burned by

112

the Oregon volunteers, Nov. 14, 1855, Rev. L. N. St. Onge and J. B. Boulet undertook its rebuilding. The history of this mission from this second founding was the familiar tale of surmounting frontier obstacles on the road to final stability, prosperity and recognition as a city parish.

53. *Personal Memoirs of P. H. Sheridan*, I: 62-63; Nesmith to Curry, Dalles of the Columbia, Nov. 19, 1855, in *Weekly Oregonian*, Dec. 1, 1855, p. 2; Haller, "Memorandum connected with a Scout," Nov. 11, Nov. 12, 1855, Ms. *UofW*; William Charles Painter, "Journal," Nov. 14, 1855, Typescript. *WHS*.

54. Rains to Cooper, Fort Vancouver, Dec. 1, 1855, *NA: RG* 94; Nesmith to Curry, Dalles of the Columbia, Nov. 19, 1855, *OHS*.

55. Haller, "Memorandum connected with a Scout," Nov. 16, 1855, Ms. *UofW*; Waman C. Hembree, "Diary," Nov. 16, 1855, Typescript, *WHS*.

56. A. V. Wilson to Nesmith, Dalles, O.T., Nov. 19, 1855, in *Weekly Oregonian*, Nov. 24, 1855, p. 2; J. K. Kelly to Curry, Dalles, O.T. Nov. 14, 1855, *OrA*; Wilson insisted in his report to Nesmith, Nov. 19, 1855, that in weather as adverse as had plagued them, they were fortunate to have lost only: 1 keg of vinegar, 21 pack saddles, 1,600 lbs of flour, 350 lbs of peas, 2 boxes of soap, 25 lbs of saleratus [baking soda], 100 lbs of sugar, 2 sacks of salt, 4 parfleches, and 16 pack animals. *Weekly Oregonian*, Nov. 24, 1855, p. 2.

57. *idem*.

58. Nesmith to Curry, Dalles of the Columbia, Nov. 19, 1855, in *Weekly Oregonian*, Dec. 1, 1855, p. 2; A. P. Dennison and Benj Stark to Curry, Portland, Nov. 24, 1855, in *Correspondence and Official Proceedings*, 51.

59. Nesmith to Curry, Dalles, O.T., Nov. 26, 1855, in *Correspondence and Official Proceedings*, 56.

60. Nesmith to Curry, Fort Dalles, O.T., Oct. 22, 1855, in *ibid.*, p. 19; Nesmith to Curry, Cascades, W.T., Oct. 18, 1855, in *ibid.*, p. 17; Nesmith to Curry, Fort Dalles, O.T., Nov. 3, 1855, in *ibid.*, p. 33; Nesmith to Curry, Dalles of the Columbia, Nov. 19, 1855, *OHS*: Absalom J. Hembree to Herman H. Snow, Fort Dalles, Nov. 21, 1855, Ms. No. 289, *OHS*: Wasco to editor, from Dalles, O.T., Nov. 1, 1855, *Weekly Oregonian*, Nov. 10, 1855, p. 2; Jon to T. J. Dryer, Dalles, O.T., Oct. 30, 1855, in *ibid.*, Nov. 3, 1855, p. 2; *Oregon Weekly Times*, Dec. 8, 1855, p. 2; *Oregon Statesman*, Dec. 8, 1855, p. 2; *Weekly Oregonian*, Dec. 8, 1855, p. 2.

61. Nesmith to Curry, Dalles of the Columbia, Nov. 19, 1855, in *Weekly Oregonian*, Dec. 1, 1855, p. 2; *Oregon Statesman*, Dec. 8, 1855, p. 2; *Oregon Weekly Times*, Dec. 8, 1855; Nesmith to Curry, Dalles, Nov. 26, 1855; same to same, Portland, Nov. 30, 1855, in *Correspondence and Official Proceedings*, 57, 59-60.

62. Curry to James K. Kelly, Dalles, O.T., Nov. 3, 1855, in *ibid.*, p. 32; same to same, Dalles, O.T., Nov. 8, 1855, in *ibid.*, p. 39.

63. Mark A. Chinn to T. J. Dryer, Dalles, O.T., Nov. 11, 1855, in *Weekly Oregonian*, Nov. 17, 1855, p. 2.

64. Narcisse Raymond to Curry, Walla Walla Country, Nov. 14, 1855; Raymond to Nathan Olney, Walla Walla Country, Nov. 14, 1855; Chinn to James K. Kelly, Well Springs Camp, Nov. 17, 1855, OrA.

65. Harvey A. Hogue to T. J. Dryer, Ft. Henrietta, O.T., Nov. 20, 1855, in *Weekly Oregonian*, Dec. 1, 1855, p. 2. Fort Henrietta (named after Mrs. Granville O. Haller), erected on the north side of the Umatilla River across from Echo, Oregon, was built of large split timbers with two bastions of round logs. Outside the hundred-foot-square stockade there was a corral made of split rails.

66. Plymptom Kelly, "Diary," Dec. 2, 1855, Ms. *CtY*.

67. *ibid.*, Dec. 5, 6, 1855, Ms. *CtY*; Davis Layton to W. H. Farrar, Dalles, O.T., June 18, 1856, *OHS*.

68. A. H. Sale, "Indian War Recollections," *Oregon Native Son*, I (1899), 336; Layton to Farrar, Dalles, O.T., June 18, 1856, *OHS*.

69. Plympton Kelly, "Diary," Dec. 7, 14, 1855, Ms. *CtY*; James Sinclair to Dr. Wm. Cowan, Ft. Vancouver, Feb. 10, 1856, Ms. Quoted by permission of the Provincial Archives, Victoria, B.C.; hereafter cited as *CaBViP*.

70. Casualties among the Volunteers in the four days of fighting were:
    Co. A
    E. B. Kelso, killed; Jesse Fleming wounded on Dec. 8, died on December 13. Capt. A. V. Wilson, Frank Duval,* and E. B. Kelsey* were wounded.
    Co. B
    Joseph Sturdevant* and G. W. Smith,* wounded.
    Co. F
    Capt. Charles Bennett, killed.
    Co. H
    Lt. J. M. Burrows,* killed. Capt. Davis Layton, Sgt. Major Isaac Miller,* Frank Crabtree,* Henry Crow,* A. M.

Addington,* T. J. Payne,* John Smith,* Casper Snook,* and Nathan Fry,* wounded.

Co. I

S. S. Van Hagerman,* killed. Capt. L. B. Munson, wounded.

Co. K

J. B. Gervais,* wounded.

An accurate count of casualties was as difficult to obtain in this instance as it usually is in a highly mobile encounter between violent partisans. Years later one of the white participants asserted that "On the battlefield we found 87 dead and in the river we found 15 and at their camp we found 12 dead Indians which had been wounded and taken to 'swet houses' where they had died." These figures, in the event of their being correct, total 114 dead. A. B. Roberts, "The Yakima War of 1855 . . . ," *Clark County History,* 8 (1967), 238.

71. B. F. Dowell to Samuel Dowell,* Esq., Fort Dalles, O.T., Dec. 23, 1855, Ms. *CUB:* Mark Chinn to Curry, Jan. 4, 1856, Ms. *OrA;* Cornelius to his wife, Whitman's, W.T., Nov. 27, 1855, Ms. *CSmH; Weekly Oregonian,* Dec. 29, 1855, p. 2; James K. Kelly to Curry, Dalles, O.T., Dec. 27, 1855, *OrA.*

72. Nesmith to Curry, Dalles, O.T., Nov. 26, 1855: same to same, Portland, Nov. 30, 1855, in *Correspondence and Official Proceedings,* 57, 59-60.

73. Cornelius to his wife, Whitman's Station, Nov. 19, 1855, Ms. Quoted by permission of the Henry E. Huntington Library and Art Gallery; cited as *CSmH.* Farrar to Curry, Dalles of the Columbia, Dec. 10, 1855, in *Correspondence and Official Proceedings,* 67.

74. James M. Campbell, "The Campbell Family," in Earle Richardson, ed., *Polk County Pioneer Sketches,* (Dallas, Oregon, Polk County, Itemizer-Observer, 1929) II: p. 10.

75. Plympton Kelly, "Diary," Dec. 11, 1855, Ms. *CtY.*

76. Narcisse Raymond to John F. Noble, Pashresh, Dec. 22, 1855: same to same, Mission Claim, Jan. 13, 1856, Ms. *UofO;* John F. Noble to Lloyd Brooke, Dalles, O.T., Dec. 19, 1855, in *Weekly Oregonian,* Dec. 29, 1856, p. 1; Chinn to Curry, Camp Curry, Jan. 4, 1856, Ms. *OrA.*

77. Plympton Kelly, "Diary," Dec. 12, 1855, Ms. *CtY.* The book was, James D. Dana, *Manual of Minerology including observations on Mines, Rocks, Reduction of Ores, and the Applications of the Science to the Arts.* (New Haven, Durrie and Peck, 1849.)

78. Plympton Kelly, "Diary," Dec. 16, 1855, Ms. *CtY.*

79. *ibid.*, Dec. 17, 1855, Ms. *CtY*; Curry to R. R. Thompson, Portland, Dec. 27, 1855, Ms. *OHS*: Chirouse to Mesplie, Tamalinla, Jan. 15, 1856, Ms. *NA: RG* 94; Stanley S. Spaid, "Joel Palmer and Indian Affairs in Oregon," (Ph. D. Dissertation, University of Oregon, Eugene, 1950) p. 199.

80. Cornelius to his wife [Florentine], Whitman Station, W.T., Dec. 19, 1855: same to same, Whitmans, W.T., Nov. 27, 1855, Ms. *CSmH*.

81. Plymptom Kelly, "Diary," Jan. 24, 28, 1856, Ms. *CtY*; See also, Curry to Cornelius, Salem, Jan. 13, 1856, Ms. *OHS*: Special Order No. 2, Headquarters Regiment, OMV, Camp Mill Creek, Jan. 28, 1856, "Regimental Order Book, First Regiment, Oregon Mounted Volunteers, Col. T. R. Cornelius, Commdg." Ms. *WaSp*; A. H. Sale, "Indian War Recollections, *Oregon Native Son*, I (1899), 389, 390; E. M. Barnum to Cornelius, Salem, Jan. 23, 1856, Ms. *CSmH*.

82. Frances Fuller Victor, *The Early Indian Wars of Oregon Compiled from the Oregon Archives and other Original Sources with Muster Rolls* (Salem, Frank C. Baker, State Printer, 1894) p. 455; Curry to Cornelius, Dalles, Feb. 15, 1856, Ms. *OHS*: Elwood Evans, *History of the Pacific Northwest: Oregon and Washington* (2 vols., Portland, North Pacific History Co., 1889) I: 538; Cornelius to his wife, Whitmans Station, W.T., Jan. 12, 1856, Ms. *CSmH*.

83. A. V. Wilson to Nesmith, Dalles, O.T., Nov. 19, 1855, in *Weekly Oregonian*, Nov. 24, 1855, p. 2; Wilson to Cornelius, Fort Henrietta, Jan. 31, 1856, Ms. *CSmH*; *Weekly Oregonian*, Feb. 9, 1856, p. 2.

84. Cornelius to John F. Miller, Camp Mill Creek, Feb. 1, 1856: Cornelius to R. R. Thompson, Camp Mill Creek, Feb. 1, 1856, "Reg. Order Book," *WaSp*.

85. Wilson to Cornelius, Fort Henrietta, Jan. 31, 1856, Ms. *CSmH*: (Special Order No. 38) Fort Henrietta, Feb. 20, 1856, in "Reg. Order Book," *WaSp*; Cornelius to Curry, Camp Cornelius, March 8, 1856, Ms. *OrA*.

86. Special Order No. 42, Camp Cornelius, Feb. 27, 1856: (Special Order No. 50), Camp Cornelius, March 6, 1856, in "Reg. Order Book," *WaSp*.

87. Special Order No. 16, Camp Mill Creek, Feb. 4, 1856, in *ibid.*, *WaSp*; Cornelius to Curry, Camp Cornelius, March 8, 1856. *OrA*.

88. Special Order No. 31, Camp Cornelius, Feb. 15, 1856: Special Order No. 40, Camp Cornelius, Feb. 26, 1856: Cornelius to Lt. J. H. Smith,* Co. D, Camp Cornelius, Feb. 28, 1856: Cornelius to Capt. A. Rivais, Camp Tuchet, March 10, 1856, in "Reg. Order Book," *WaSp*; Cornelius to Curry, Camp Cornelius, March 8, 1856, Ms. *OrA.*

89. Curry to Cornelius, Portland, March 15, 1856, Ms. *OHS.*

90. Special Order No. 43, Camp Cornelius, Feb. 27, 1856, in "Reg. Order Book," *WaSp*; Plympton Kelly, "Diary," March 5, 1856, Ms. *CtY.*

91. Special Order No. 48, Camp Cornelius, March 5, 1856, "Reg. Order Book," *WaSp;* Plympton Kelly, "Diary," March 5, 1856, *CtY.*

92. Cornelius to his wife, Whitman Station, Feb. 6, 1856, *CSmH*; General Order, Camp Cornelius, March 5, 1856: Cornelius to W. H. Fauntleroy, Camp Cornelius, March 6, 1856: same to same, Camp Palluse Falls, March 22, 1856, "Reg. Order Book," *WaSp.*

93. General Order, Camp Cornelius, March 7, 1856: Cornelius to Lt. C. B. Pillow, Camp Cornelius, March 8, 1856: Cornelius to W. H. Fauntleroy, Camp Cornelius, March 8, 1856: Special Order, Camp Mouth [of the] Yakima, March 31, 1856. "Reg. Order Book," *WaSp.*

94. General Order, Camp Cornelius, March 8, 1856, *ibid., WaSp.*

95. Cornelius to Curry, Camp Yakima, April 2, 1856, in *Weekly Oregonian*, April 12, 1856, p. 2.

96. Plympton Kelly, "Diary," March 18, 1856: March 20, 1856, Ms. *OHS*; General Order, Camp Palluse Falls, March 20, 1856, "Reg. Order Book," *WaSp*; T. J. Small to T. A. Wood, Jefferson, Mo., Jan. 29, 1899, in *Oregon Native Son*, I (1899), p. 92; J. Orin Oliphant, ed., "Journals of the Indian War 1855-56" Journal of Robert M. Painter, *WHQ*, 15 (1924), p. 23; James K. Kelly, "Memo Book," March 20, 22, 1856, Ms. *OHS.*

97. Shiel made his presentation in a series of pointed questions that found their mark. He asked the mutineers if they supposed that this was a fishing expedition. Then, he recalled the more recent Indian atrocities that had led to this war, mentioning the Whitman Massacre, the murder of A. J. Bolon, the defeat of Major Haller's force, and the battlefield deaths of Charles Bennett and E. B. Kelso. Against this background, he asked whether this was the time to turn back, thus leaving the In-

dians in victorious possession of the land. His final query was whether it was better to fight the Indians in their own country or wait until they burst upon the settlements and devastated the homes of white people. A. H. Sale, "Indian War Recollections," *Oregon Native Son*, I: (1899), 390.

98. Cornelius to Curry, Camp Yakima, April 2, 1856, in *Weekly Oregonian*, April 12, 1856, p. 2.

99. Special Order, Camp Collumbia river, March 29, 1856, "Reg. Order Book," *WaSp*; Plympton Kelly, "Diary," March 30, 1856, Ms. *OHS*; Cornelius to Curry, Camp Yakima, April 2, 1856, in *Weekly Oregonian*, April 12, 1856; Special Order No. [ ], Camp Opposite Fort Walla Walla, Apprile 6, 1856, "Reg. Order Book," *WaSp*.

100. Wright to David R. Jones, Fort Dalles, March 12, 1856, Ms. *NA:RG* 393; James J. Archer to his sister [Nannie], Cascades, Washington Territory, March 30, 1856. Ms. *MD*.

101. Wright to David R. Jones, Camp at the Cascades of the Columbia River, W.T., April 4, 1856: Wallen to Hodges, Fort Vancouver, March 31, 1856. *NA: RG* 393; F. M. Sebring, "The Indian Raids on the Cascades in March, 1856," *WHQ*, XIX (1928), p. 101. An undetermined number of Indians attacked the upper landing, the blockhouse, and the lower landing at the Cascades, March 26, 1856. The attackers were finally driven off by nightfall, March 27, leaving 14 whites dead, as well as four Indians, with 22 whites injured, and most of the buildings in ashes.

102. Archer to his sister [Nannie], Fort Vancouver, April 10, 1856: Archer to his mother, Fort Vancouver, April 12, 1856, Ms. *MD*; David Blaine to his family, Portland, March 19, 1856, Ms. *CSmH*; K. A. Peterson* to James Birnie & Co., Portland, Jan. 23, 1856. Ms. No. 920, *OHS*.

103. Cornelius to Curry, Camp Yakima, April 2, 1856, in *Weekly Oregonian*, April 12, 1856, p. 2; same to same, Dalles of the Columbia, April 13, 1856, in *ibid.*, April 19, 1856, p. 2; Plympton Kelly, "Diary," April 6, 7, 8, 1856, Ms. *OHS*; General Order, Camp Yackama, W.T., Aprile 7, 1856, "Reg. Order Book," *WaSp*. The total territorial vote was 4,186 in favor of a constitutional convention and 4,435 opposed. The measure lost by 249 votes. Charles H. Carey, *The Oregon Constitution and Debates of the Constitutional Convention of 1857* (Salem, State Printing Dept., 1926), 20.

104. Plympton Kelly, "Diary," April 10, 1856, Ms. *OHS*; Oliphant, ed., Journal of Robert M. Painter, *WHQ*, 15 (1924), p. 24; Cornelius to his wife, Dalles, O.T., April 14, 1856, Ms. *CSmH*.

105. V. W. Schaeffer to his mother, Portland, O.T., May 11, 1856, Ms. No. 1086, *OHS*: A. P. Ankeny to T. J. Dryer, Camp Opposite Walla Walla, April 5, 1856: D to Dryer, Camp on Clickitat, April 11, 1856, in *Weekly Oregonian*, April 19, 1856, p. 2; Cornelius to Curry, Camp Yakima, April 2, 1856, in *ibid.*, April 12, 1856, p. 2; Cornelius to his wife, Dalles, O.T., April 16, 1856, Ms. *CSmH*; Hiram Wilber to Curry, Camp 5 miles from the Dalls, April 21, 1856, Ms. *OrA*.

106. Cornelius to Curry, Camp Yakima, April 2, 1856, in *Weekly Oregonian*, April 12, 1856, p. 2; Ankeny to Dryer, Camp Opposite Walla Walla, April 5, 1856; same to same, Camp Canyon Creek, April 10, 1856, in *ibid.*, April 19, 1856, p. 2; Wilber to Curry, Camp 5 miles from the Dalls, April 21, 1856, Ms. *OrA*.

107. Curry to John McCracken, AQM Genl., Portland, April 12, 1856; Curry to J. Curl, Portland, April 12, 1856; Curry to Cornelius, Portland, April, 1856; Curry to Lt. Col. Kelly, Portland, April 16, 1856. Ms. *UofO*.

108. Farrar to Deady, Camp Dalles, May 2, 1856. Ms. *OHS*.

109. Curry to McCarver, Portland, April 21, 1856, Ms. *UofO*; Plympton Kelly, "Diary," April 26, 1856. Ms. *OHS*; M. M. McCarver to the editor, Portland, May 16, 1856, in *Oregon Weekly Times*, May 24, 1856, p. 2.

110. Oliphant, ed., Journal of Robert M. Painter, *WHQ*, XV (1924), 26; W. H. Farrar to Lt. Col. Kelly, Camp Dalles, April 30, 1856, Ms. *OHS*; Henry Hill* to James Hill, Independence, O.T., May 11, 1856. Ms. *UofO*.

111. James K. Kelly to Davis Layton, Fort Henrietta, April 23, 1856. Ms. *OHS*.

112. Wright to Curry, Camp at Fort Dalles, O.T., April 27, 1856, in *Journal of the House of Representatives of the Territory of Oregon: Appendix*. (Salem, Public Printer, 1856), 45; Gov. G. L. Curry, General Order No. 30, Portland, April 28, 1856, *OHS*: R. R. Thompson to George Wright, Dalles, April 26, 1856, in *House Journal: Appendix*, 45.

113. Cornelius to Lt. Col. J. Kelly, Dalles, O.T., April 30, 1856, *OHS*. The activities of Wright and of the Oregon Rangers are not within the scope of Plympton Kelly's diary.

114. "Muster Roll, Co. E, Recruiting Battalion, First Regiment, OMV, Capt. Wm. A. Cason, March 1-May 30, 1856.": "Muster Roll,

Co. K, First Regiment, OMV, Capt. Antoine Rivais *vice* Capt.
N. A. Cornoyer, Oct. 30, 1855-May 31, 1856, *OHS*; Cornelius to
Wilson, Camp Dalles, O.T., April 30, 1856, "Reg. Order Book,"
*WaSp*; "Return of Capt. A. V. Wilson, Co. A, First Regiment,
OMV, for the Month of May 1856," *OrA*.

115. *Weekly Oregonian*, May 10, 1856, p. 2.

116. Cornelius to his wife, Dalles, O.T., April 16, 1856. *CSmH*.

117. The steamer *Multnomah* landed at Oregon City, June 1851 and
ran up the Willamette River until she was taken around the
falls in May 1852 to run between Oregon City and Portland. In
the fall of 1852, under Capt. W. H. Fauntleroy, she was placed
on the Portland-Cascades route. The following year, with
Capt. Richard Hoyt commanding, she returned to the Oregon
City-Portland route until 1854, when she was assigned to
transporting the U.S. Mail to Astoria.

118. The basic sources on the Kelly clan are, Richmond Kelly, *The
Kelly Clan* (Portland, The Author, 1901): and Laura Kelly and
Esther Kelly Watson, *The Kelly Family*, 2 Pts., (Portland,
Privately Printed, 1973). Supplemental information concern-
ing a family as prominent as this one in Oregon affairs may be
found in: "Plympton J. Kelly," *Oregon Native Son*, 1 (1899):
Joseph Gaston, *Portland Oregon Its History and Builders*, 3
vols., (Chicago, S. J. Clarke Publishing, 1911), II: 660; Joseph
Gaston, *The Centennial History of Oregon*, 3 vols. (Chicago, S.
J. Clarke Publishing Co., 1912), III: 373; *Portrait and Bio-
graphical Record of Portland and Vicinity Oregon* (Chicago,
Chapman Publishing Co., 1903), 607-608. Manuscript materials
hold some rewards for the patient searcher. For example,
Indian War Pension Paper #0606, *OHS*; muster rolls for the
various companies of Volunteers and Rangers and Papers of
the Provisional and Territorial government of Oregon, #2143,
5477, 5707, 6915, and 9101, *OrA*; and the "Regimental Order
Book First Regt. of Oregon Mounted Volunteers Thomas R.
Cornelius Col. Commndg Reg. Wm. H. Farrar Adjutant of
Regiment," Ms., *WaSp*. Local newspapers had recurring
references to different members of the family as those noting
Plympton Kelly's passing: "Plympton Kelly," *Oregon Sunday
Journal*, Sept. 16, 1906, p. 9, column 3-4; "Aged Pioneer Dead,"
*Sunday Oregonian*, Sept. 16, 1906, p. 32, column 2-3; "Funeral
of Plympton Kelly," *Morning Oregonian*, Sept. 17, 1906, p. 7,
column 4.

119. Co. A had returned to The Dalles, Nov. 19, 1855, and was ordered to the Walla Walla Country with Co. I, Benton County, First Regiment, OMV, Lyman B. Munson, cmdg., and Co. K, Marion County, First Regiment, OMV, Narcisse A. Cornoyer, cmdg. The 180 man force was enroute to reinforce Major Mark Chinn even before his appeal for additional troops arrived. A. V. Wilson to J. W. Nesmith, The Dalles, Nov. 19, 1855 in *Weekly Oregonian*, Nov. 24, 1855, p. 2; J. W. Nesmith to Curry, Dalles of the Columbia, O.T., Nov. 19, 1855 in *Correspondence and Official Proceedings*, 46.

120. They were following the common route from the Dalles to the Walla Walla Valley that was simply the Oregon Trail through modern Miller, Biggs, Rock Creek, Cecil, Well Springs, and Butter Creek to the Umatilla River near Stanfield. The Walla Walla trail angled northeastward from the Umatilla across Cold Springs and Juniper canyons and over the high ridges into the vicinity of Whitman's former mission.

121. Chinn's command had left The Dalles Nov. 12 and was encamped at Wells Springs when Narcisse Raymond's message was delivered. The news that Peu-Peu-Mox-Mox, with a thousand warriors, was occupying the hills around Ft. Walla Walla was sufficient to make Chinn halt at the Umatilla River where he built Ft. Henrietta, in which he awaited reinforcements. F. F. Victor, *The Early Indian Wars of Oregon*, 439; Mark Chinn to James K. Kelly, Wells Springs Camp, Nov. 17, 1855, *OrA*.

122. The observation is valid as 234 are known to have died on the trail during the emigration of 1852. This frightening toll reflected the estimated 12 to 15,000 emigrants of that year.

123. Juniper is a small evergreen shrub or tree of the pine family. Prickly pear is the pear-shaped fruit of a number of flat-stemmed cactuses.

124. Major Chinn's command was comprised of Co. B, Wasco County, First Regiment, OMV, Orlando Humason, cmdg.; Co. H, Linn County, First Regiment, OMV, Davis Layton, cmdg.; and Co. I, Benton County, First Regiment, OMV, Lyman, B. Munson, cmdg.

125. This wagon was presented to the regiment by Mrs. Granville Haller when it proved impossible to procure a suitable ambulance conveyance at The Dalles.

126. Ft. Walla Walla was built originally as Ft. Nez Perce by the North West Company in 1818, "was rebuilt once or possibly

twice during the period from 1820 to 1832," and rebuilt with adobe bricks after burning down, Oct. 5, 1841. Thomas E. Garth," Archeological Excavations at Fort Walla Walla," *PNQ*, 43 (1952), 32. Quoted by permission of the University of Washington.

127. The loss included 400 lbs T P F gunpowder and 1008 lbs ball thrown into the Columbia River in the presence of witnesses by order of Nathan Olney, Oct. 13, 1855. George Simpson explained in a later letter that Sinclair's evaluation of $20,000 was evidently prepared "as the foundation of a claim on the U.S. Government . . . The supposed value of the fort itself may be about the proper mark, but that is merely nominal, as Walla Walla was one of the posts I intended to propose being abandoned in consequence of its unprofitableness." Nathan Olney "Receipt for Hudson's Bay Company property destroyed at Fort Walla Walla, W.T., 13 October 1855" (All/71/602): George Simpson to W. G. Smith, Secty to the Co., Hudson's Bay House, Lachine, 28 January 1856 (A12/8/11), *HBC*.

128. Greasewood is a shrubby, stiff, prickly plant found growing in alkaline soils.

129. Co. B, Wasco County, "commanded by Lts. John Jeffreys and James McCaulif. Captain O. Humason was at home [The Dalles] in bed, sick." Co. H, Linn County, Capt. Lyman B. Munson, cmdg. "Amos Underwood's Story of the Capture and Death of Peu-Peu-Mox-Mox," *Ladd & Bush Quarterly*, 2 (1914), 4.

130. Capt. Charles Bennett (1811-1855), Co. F, Marion County, First Regiment, OMV; Lt. John M. Burrows* (c. 1828-1855), Co. H, Linn County, First Regiment, OMV; Pvt. E. B. Kelso (c. 1831-1855), Co. A, Multnomah County, First Regiment, OMV; Pvt. Henry Crow* (c. 1827-1855), Co. H, Linn County, First Regiment, OMV, was wounded on Dec. 7 and died the next day.

131. The severest fighting took place near the LaRocque cabin, some four miles beyond Dry Creek, two miles below Whitman's mission site, and nine miles west of Walla Walla. John Burrows* died here. Companies A and F pushed the Indians about a mile and a half up the Walla Walla River where they occupied the Tellier* cabin, "from which they could not be easily driven." Here Charles Bennett and E. B. Kelso were killed. LaRocque's* house served as a hospital to which the

122

wounded and dead were carried. T. C. Elliott, "The Murder of Peu-Peu-Mox-Mox," *OHQ*, 35 (1934), 127-28; F. F. Victor, *The Early Indian Wars of Oregon, 443-44;* Frank T. Gilbert, *Historic Sketches of Walla Walla, Whitman, Columbia, and Garfield Counties, Washington and Umatilla County, Oregon* (Portland, A. G. Walling, 1885), 181.

132. The explosion burned Wilson's face. James K. Kelly to W. H. Farrar, Fort Bennett, Dec. 14, 1855, in *Weekly Oregonian,* Jan. 5, 1856, p. 2.

133. Co. D, Washington County, Capt. Thomas R. Cornelius, cmdg., and Co. E, Yamhill County, Capt. A. J. Hembree, cmdg. These two companies marched through the night from Ft. Henrietta to bring the requested succor. "Muster Roll, Co. D, First Regiment, OMV, Oct. 19, 1855-May 5, 1856." "Muster Roll, Co. E, First Regiment, OMV, Oct. 19, 1855-May 7, 1856," Ms. *OrA.*

134. Co. K, Marion County, Capt. Narcisse Cornoyer, cmdg., "Came to white settlements on Touchet, settlers [were] forted up with about 100 friendly Indians — escorted them to Camp Curry . . ." Muster Roll, Co. K, First Regiment, OMV, Oct. 30, 1855-May 31, 1856," Ms. *OrA.*

135. Brooke, Bomford, and Noble's buildings on their Touchet River claim were new and well-constructed of hewn logs. "Testimony of H. M. Chase, May 21, 1896," Indian Depredation Case #2117, U.S. Court of Claims Records, *NA: RG* 123.

136. This vandalism did not go unchallenged, as is clear from the report that "the Wasco boys Co. B were for pitching into the party, for breaking open the trunks and stealing our things, as most of them knew us well." John F. Noble to Lloyd Brooke, Dalles, O.T., Dec. 19, 1855, in *Weekly Oregonian,* Dec. 29, 1855, p. 2.

137. The grisly spectacle was not universally approved as one caustic observer made clear in his recollection that "I took a walk about our camp and found that the brave boys who had, as was their custom stayed at home, had taken Peo-Peo-Mox-Mox and his companions who had been hurriedly thrown into an old cache when killed — and lightly covered with some old straw and trash — and had dragged them some distance from the fort or stockade and promptly scalped them." A. B. Roberts, "The Yakima War etc.," *Clark County History,* 8 (1967), 238-39. Quoted by permission of the Fort Vancouver Historical Society.

138. Roberts would recall later that "Soon after, and while hunting one day near the old Whitman Mission I found a large hand mill, which was taken to camp and made very useful in grinding corn and wheat which we found in considerable quantities in various caches . . ." A. B. Roberts, "Account of the Yakima War." Ms. *OHS*.

139. Whitman's Mission was located at Waiilatpu (the place of rye grass) some 25 miles up the Walla Walla River from its mouth. Marcus Whitman finished the first rough cabin by Dec. 9, 1836 and had 16 acres under cultivation in 1837. The mission compound and fields expanded during the next ten years to the increased relief of each year's emigrants and the mounting suspicion of neighboring Indians. The hard-earned permanence of the mission fields and buildings helped incite the massacre of 14 people, Nov. 29, 1847.

140. The new location was Camp Curry, named in honor of Gov. George L. Curry.

141. The French settlers and friendly Indians moved to their camp on Mill Creek, about ten miles from the Whitman Mission ruins, on Dec. 18, 1855. Co. K, Marion County, was assigned to protect these people from Dec. 18 until Feb. 29, 1856. Chinn to Curry, Camp Curry, Jan. 4, 1856; "Muster Roll, Co. K, First Regiment, OMV, Oct. 30, 1855-May 31, 1856." Ms. *OrA*.

142. William H. Fauntleroy was the Asst. Regimental Quartermaster and Commissary.

143. Nesmith, on leave of absence, reached Portland, Dec. 1, and resigned from the Volunteers, Dec. 4, 1855, with the explanation "that this has been necessary because of sickness in my family, together with urgent and important private business." The questionable validity of these published reasons is underscored by his adjutant, Wm. H. Farrar, viewing the departure as, "this unexpected event." Curry to Nesmith, On Board Steamboat *Enterprise*, Nov. 26, 1855, in *Correspondence and Official Proceedings*, 53; *Weekly Oregonian*, Dec. 1, 1855, p. 2; Farrar to Curry, Dalles of the Columbia, O.T., Dec. 10, 1855, in *Correspondence and Official Proceedings*, 67; *Oregon Weekly Times*, Dec. 8, 1855.

144. James K. Kelly arrived in Portland, Jan. 9, 1856, after a five day hike from The Dalles. The entire trip by foot was made "on the south side and along the bank of the Columbia river, a feat we believe never before accomplished by white men." Kelly attended the sessions of the Legislative Assembly in Salem from

Jan. 12 to adjournment, Jan. 31, 1856. *Weekly Oregonian*, Jan. 12, 1856, p. 2; *Journal of the Council of the Legislative Assembly of the Territory of Oregon during the Seventh Regular Session From Dec. 3, 1855 to Jan. 31, 1856*, 63, 186.

145 Isaac I. Stevens' accomplishment in reaching the Volunteers' camp in the dead of winter was notable. He and his party left the Blackfoot Council Grounds, near Ft. Benton on the upper Missouri River, after completing a treaty with these Indians, Oct. 24, 1855. Four days later, October 28, the party moved out of the council site and were 35 miles along the trail when met the next day by Wm. H. Pearson, tireless expressman, with the news that the interior tribes of Washington were on the warpath. A more adequately armed party made a second start from Ft. Benton, October 31, reached Ft. Owen in the Flathead country by November 4, left there on November 14 and in an exhausting winter crossing crested the Bitterroot Mountains November 20 to reach Sacred Heart Mission among the Coeur d'Alene Indians on November 24. He pushed ahead to Antoine Plante's ferry on the Spokane River where he held a council with the Spokane tribe, December 3-5, before leaving for Wm. Craig's home among the friendly Nez Perce that was reached safely, December 11. With an escort of 100 Nez Perces, 50 miners returning from the Colville district and his own party he reached the Walla Walla country. No one has ever challenged the courage and stamina manifested in this long trip through hostile land at the worst time of the year. Hazard Stevens, *Isaac Ingalls Stevens*, II: 120-47.

146. The severity of the weather was noted repeatedly by different Volunteers and the current newspapers. B. F. Dowell to Sam'l Dowell, Esq.*, Fort Dalles, Dec. 25, 1855. Ms. *CtY*; Cornelius to his wife, Whitman's, W.T., Nov. 27, 1855, Ms. *CSmH*; James K. Kelly to Curry, Dalles, O.T., Dec. 27, 1855, Ms. *OrA*; *Weekly Oregonian*, Dec. 29, 1855, p. 2; Chinn to Curry, Camp Curry, Jan. 4, 1856, Ms. *OrA*.

147. Although Gov. Curry would stoutly defend the Volunteers' conduct against the sharp allegations of Col. George Wright a few months later, it is impossible to disregard the plain evidence of marauding, thievery and vandalism contained in the diary entries for Dec. 12, 16, 17 and 21. Geo. L. Curry to Col. George Wright, Portland, May 13, 1856 in *House Journal, 1855-1856, Appendix*, 46.

148. Despite missing the significance of what he was witnessing,

Plympton faithfully noted the key incidents in the unfortunate Chinn-Cornelius squabble over Cornelius's right to command. Cf., entries for Dec. 19, Jan. 4, 24 and 28.

149. The new site, some two miles up Mill Creek at the edge of the timber, was named Camp Mill Creek.

150. Co. H, Linn County, Capt. Davis Layton, cmdg.; Co. I, Benton County, Capt. Lyman B. Munson, cmdg.

151. The Indian prisoners were: Howlish Wampoo,* a Cayuse chief; Tim-Tim-mit-see,* Stickus,* and also the prisoners Was-as-tee-mee-nee or Painted Earth,* a brother of Howlish Wampoo; Sta-how-ee, or McKays*; Too-too-na-tash-whit,* a half Nez Perce and Cayuse and a son-in-law of Stickus; Tick-i-us-us, a son of Stickus; and Tock or Potato Heap.* "Report by Board of Investigation, Camp Mill Creek, Jan. 28, 1856" in "Reg. Order Book," *WaSp.*

152. Capt. A. J. Hembree, with a detachment of 31 men, "captured 300 wild Indian horses while on a scout from Jan. 15 to 24, 1856." "Muster Roll, Co. E, First Regiment, OMV, Oct. 19, 1855-May 7, 1856." Ms. *OrA.*

153. Cornelius was elected colonel of the First Regiment replacing James Nesmith, Dec. 18, 1855. He assumed command on Jan. 4, 1856, although Maj. Mark Chinn refused to recognize his authority because Gov. Curry had not sent an official commission confirming the election. A. H. Sale, "Indian War Recollections," *Oregon Native Son,* I (1899), 389.

154. Chinn was suspended from his command and given permission to return home. Ten days later he was restored to duty. He was not elected first major to fill the office vacated by the resignation of Major Ambrose N. Armstrong,* Dec. 27, 1855. Apparently, Plympton Kelly's expression of indignation, so interesting in the light of his November 29 entry, did not reflect the attitude of the regiment which eventually elected Capt. Narcisse Cornoyer, Co. K, to fill the empty post. Curry to Armstrong, Portland, O.T., Dec. 27, 1855, Ms. No. 367, No. 700, *OHS;* E. M. Barnum to Cornelius, Jan. 23, 1856, Ms. *CSmH;* Cornelius to R. R. Thompson, Camp Mill Creek, Jan. 28, 1856 in "Reg. Order Book," *WaSp.*

155. "You will immediately inspect the men, horses, and arms in your respective commands, and in writing report to the Adjutant of the Regt., specifically concerning each, as to condition, fitness &c." General Order No. 1, Camp Mill Creek, Jan. 28, 1856 in "Reg. Order Book," *WaSp.*

156. The Board of Investigation appointed to examine the Indians held at Co. K's Camp Cornoyer, Jan. 28, 1856, was made up of Lt. Chas. B. Pillow, Co. A; Lt. Wm. G. Haley,* Co. H, Lt. Thos. J. Small, Co. K, and Wm. H. Farrar as Judge Advocate. The Board found that "*Wat-as-tu-mu-nu* or *Painted Earth,** and *Tock* or *Potato Heap** were engaged in the battle of Walla Walla and discharged their firearms at the whites: fled to Nez Perces country; *Lawyer,** Nez Perces chief, advised them to surrender; *Tock* surrendered on the morning of January 21st and *Wat-as-tu-mu-nu* on the 24th inst at Camp Cornoyer. They had not acted as spies. The Board recommended they be sent to the Governor of Oregon to be held as prisoners of war until the end of hostilities. *Sta-how-ee* or *McKay** was on the battlefield on December 8 did not fire on the whites. The Board recommended his transfer to the Governor of Oregon for retention until the end of the war. *Tick-i-us-us** and *Too-Too-na-tash-wit** should be restrained from returning to the Nez Perces country and kept in camp under careful watch." "Reg. Order Book," *WaSp.*

Cornelius approved the recommendations of the Board and ordered Cornoyer to deliver three prisoners (not two as the diary entry notes) *i.e., Wat-as-tu-mu-nu* or *Painted Earth, Sta-how-ee* or *McKay,* and *Tock* or *Potato Heap* to Lt. A. Hanan of Co. H, who is to "safely conduct them to His Excellency, Geo. L. Curry, Govr of Oregon, to whom you will surrender them." The regimental quartermaster was to provide transportation for three Indians, Hanan, and an escort of 19 men.

Cornelius informed Curry in a separate letter that "*Wat-as-tu-mu-nu* or *Painted Earth* is a brother of the Chief of the Cayuse Indians. It has been represented to me that he is a 'medicine man,' and that class of persons is somewhat notoriously bad. *McKay* has considerable influence amongst his people. *Tock* is a miserable specimen of the river Indians. He understands the English language in a small degree." Special Order No. 9, Camp Mill Creek, Jan. 31, 1856; Special Order No. 10, Camp Mill Creek, Jan. 31, 1856; Cornelius to Curry, Camp Mill Creek, Jan. 31, 1856, in "Reg. Order Book," *WaSp.*

157. The new camp a mile and a half farther up Mill Creek was named Camp Cornelius in honor of the regimental commander.

158. "You will procure the howitzer cached at Camp Curry; bring it into camp; mount it upon a pair of strong wheels, and have it

127

thoroughly cleaned and prepared for efficient service." Cornelius to D. H. Lownsdale, Asst. Regtal Qr. Master, Special Order No. 16, Camp Mill Creek, Feb. 4, 1856 in "Reg. Order Book," *WaSp*. Diary entries on Feb. 10 and 13 attest to the dispatch and success with which this order was executed.

159. "You will immediately make arrangements for and proceed to build six boats of a size and strength sufficient to enable me to cross my command over Snake or Columbia rivers, and will have the same completed at the earliest date possible." Cornelius to D. H. Lownsdale, A. Reg. QM, Camp Mill Creek, Feb. 4, 1856. Special Order No. 16 in *ibid.*, *WaSp*. Diary entries for Feb. 11, 29, and March 1, trace the progress of this specific preparation for renewed combat.

160. Corp. Jesse T. Bowles, Pvts. W. S. Buckley and Henry Neeves,* all of Co. A, had been tried for "disobedience of orders, neglect of duty, and general insubordination" because they refused to fall into company line at roll call and refused "to work in the construction of a corral." "Report of Regimental Court Martial per General Order No. 6," Camp Cornelius, Feb. 11, 1856 in *ibid. WaSp*.

General Order No. 5, Camp Cornelius, Feb. 9, 1856 set the stage for this trial by ordering that "The commanding officer of each Company will detail five men from his command, and order them to report in a body at the hour of nine o'clk to the officer of the day." The penalties meted out to convicted violators were to be made public to the regiment. Bowles was demoted from sergeant and deprived of all right to any future office in the regiment. The three lost all pay for ten complete days. It is interesting to note that Buckley was subsequently captain of Co. K, Oregon Mounted Rangers, April 3-June 29, 1856; and Bowles became 2nd Lt., Co. B, Oregon Mounted Rangers, May 15-June 19, 1856.

161. Lt. T. J. Small, Co. K, Marion County, was ordered to provide a suitable escort for Wm. H. Farrar, Adjt. Reg., "who will return to Camp Cornelius, having in custody certain Indian prisoners." Special Order No. 32, Camp Cannon, Feb. 16, 1856, in "Reg. Order Book," *WaSp*.

162. What developed into a minor misfortune for Plympton Kelly was set in motion Feb. 15, 1856 with Cornelius' command to Lt. B. M. Harding, Co. A, that "you will detail Corporal Kelly of your Co to take command of the escort detailed to protect Dowell's pack train from this camp to the post on the Umatil-

128

la, and thence back to Head Quarters." Special Order No. 31, Camp Cornelius, Feb. 15, 1856, in *ibid., WaSp.* Members of the escort were, Allan C. Brelsford, James B. Gentre,* Valentine W. Schaeffer, Jason A. Duvall,* John Foster,* Jacob R. John, Francis Baltimore or Noel Baltimore. "Company Return of Capt. Alfred V. Wilson, Co. A, First Regiment, OMV, for the Month of February 1856." Ms. *OrA.*

163. "Company A of the 2nd Battalion" was Co. A, Recruiting Battalion, First Regiment, OMV, Capt. E. J. Harding, cmdg., Jan. 25-May 9, 1856. This was one of the five recruiting battalions eagerly awaited by Cornelius with the expectation that "as soon as they get hear we will go and clear Mr. Indians out and will then return home." Cornelius to his wife, Whitmans Station, Feb. 6, 1856. *CSmH.*

164. The ox teams were those of Thomas Hubbard's wagon train that was under orders to proceed immediately "to Head Quarters of the Regt. in Whitman's Valley and report to D. H. Lownsdale, Asst. Regtal Qr. Master & Commissary on your arrival there." Special Order No. 39, Fort Henrietta, Feb. 20, 1856, in "Reg. Order Book," *WaSp.* The minute care exercised in apportioning the precious supplies may be inferred from the separate order given to Hubbard to "turn over three thousand pounds (3000 lbs) of flour from your load to Cyrus K. Riggs, Commissary and Quarter Master Sergt, in charge of those Departments at this post." Special Order No. 38, Fort Henrietta, Feb. 20, 1856, in *ibid., WaSp.*

165. Co. K, Marion County, Capt. Narcisse Cornoyer, cmdg.; Co. G, Polk County, Capt. Benjamin Hayden, cmdg. The successful Indian raid on the pack animals evoked an immediate order to Capt. E. J. Harding, Co. A, Recruiting Battalion, that he "send twenty-five of your best mounted men under command of a Lieutenant, or you will go yourself if you deem it advisable, in search of Dowell's pack train." Special Order No. 40, Camp Cornelius, Feb. 26, 1856, in *ibid., WaSp.*

166. Co. B, Wasco County, First Regiment, OMV, John T. Jeffries, cmdg., *vice* Orlando Humason.

167. Co. H, Linn County, Capt. Davis Layton, cmdg.; Co. E., Yamhill County. Capt. A. J. Hembree, cmdg. Two days after Plympton Kelly's escort lost the pack mules, the loss of a large number of horses from Camp Cornelius itself saw the colonel ordering Capt. Hiram Wilber to "take charge of the detachment of twenty-five men who are ordered to report ready mounted to

you in fifteen minutes time, and go in direction of Copei [Creek] in pursuit of the Indians under charge of one Tallman. You will follow the Indians until you overtake them." He further instructed the detachment to bring back not only Tallman but Howlish Wampoo, Tim-Tim-mit-see, and Stickus. The irony was that the last three named had been prisoners and were examined by the Board of Investigation, Jan. 28, 1856. Cf. Diary entry for Jan. 22. Special Order No. 43, Camp Cornelius, Feb. 27, 1856, in "Reg. Order Book," *WaSp*.

168. Lt. John H. Smith, Co. D, Washington County, was ordered to proceed to Wild Horse Creek where "you will take command of the escort to the mule train, and with all the public property return to this encampment as expeditiously as possible." Cornelius to J. H. Smith, Co. D, Camp Cornelius, Feb. 27, 1856, in *ibid., WaSp*.

169. Lt. Wm. H. Myers, Co. D, and Lt. W. H. Wright*, Co. E, Yamhill County, were ordered six days before this to "proceed to the Nez Perces country and there negotiate for the purchase of three hundred head of good serviceable riding horses from the Indians of that country." Special Order No. 42, Camp Cornelius, Feb. 27, 1856, in *ibid., WaSp*. They were able to buy only a disappointing 42 head.

170. This hurried mission to expedite any ammunition en route to the troops resulted from Cornelius's order to Lt. Wm. D. Stillwell, Co. C, Recruiting Battalion, to "take command of a detachment of ten men who are ordered to report to you at an early hour this morning. You will proceed with all reasonable expedition to meet the wagon train of Johnson, on its way here from the Dalles." He was to ascertain whether or not Johnson had powder, lead, ball and caps for the regiment. In case he did, "you will bring it directly to Hdqtrs in the lightest wagon with every possible speed. Should necessity force you to proceed to the Dalles you will procure 200 lbs lead, 15,000 percussion caps, 200 lbs fine cannister powder." Special Order, Camp Cornelius, March 5, 1856, in "Reg. Order Book," *WaSp*.

171. It is a bit puzzling that today's diary entry has no mention of the radical reduction in food consequent upon the colonel ordering the asst. commissary, W. H. Fauntleroy to "issue but one half (½) rations of flour to the troops on this (East) side of the Umatilla river." Cornelius to Fauntleroy, Camp Cornelius, March 6, 1856, in *ibid., WaSp*. The men returned from the

130

Tucannon were part of a detachment of 45 Volunteers dispatched on March 2 to escort Myers and Wright with the hoped-for 300 horses into camp. Special Order No. 45, Camp Cornelius, March 2, 1856, in *ibid.*, *WaSp.*

172. A Board of Investigation convened at Camp Cornoyer on Feb. 5, "to enquire into the conduct of a certain Indian, called Yellow Hawk." He "was hung yesterday [March 7]; he came into the friendly Indian camp in February — undoubtedly as a spy — was proved to have been an active agent of Kamiakin's, and without doubt deserved the fate he received." Special Order No. 18, Camp Mill Creek, Feb. 4, 1856, in *ibid.*, in *WaSp*; *Weekly Oregonian*, March 22, 1856, p. 2. The election of Capt. Narcisse Cornoyer as senior major opened the way for the election of Antoine Rivais to the command of Co. K.

173. The full command was under orders to march on the morning of March 9. Co. E, Yamhill County, Capt. A. J. Hembree, cmdg., was starting a day early. General Order, Camp Cornelius, March 7, 1856, in Reg. Order Book, *WaSp.* Lt. Chas. Pillow, with 50 men, was ordered to Ft. Walla Walla to establish an encampment at or near that site. He was to send out parties of scouts, search for canoes on the Columbia and Walla Walla rivers "bringing in all that are serviceable to your encampment" and destroying the remainder. The detachment was to maintain a vigilant guard and exercise every precaution against surprise. Cornelius to Lt. C. B. Pillow, Camp Cornelius, March 8, 1856, in *ibid.*, *WaSp.* This location, furthermore, was to serve as a supply camp to which Asst. Commissary W. H. Fauntleroy was to move all stores "and property whatsoever." Cornelius to Fauntleroy, Camp Cornelius, March 8, 1856, in *ibid.*, *WaSp.*

174. Co. K, Marion County, with Capt. Antoine Rivais commanding, as a result of the previous day's balloting.

175. Site of the Battle of Walla Walla, Dec. 7-10, 1855.

176. Capt. Alfred V. Wilson, Co. A, Multnomah.

177. Lt. Wm. D. Stillwell, Co. C, Recruiting Battalion, was returning from his mission to expedite the movement of ammunition to the command. Cf. March 5 diary entry.

178. The cannon was thrown into the river, Oct. 13, 1855, when all possibly useful munitions were destroyed at Ft. Walla Walla. Cf. note 127.

179. Plympton Kelly reflects the urgency of the episode in noting the prompt return of the expressmen, George Maxwell and John

Brownlee, to the Palouse Falls camp: and the supply camp at Walla Walla stirring at 3 a.m.

180. The arrival of food on March 20 took the regiment off the ½ rations that had prevailed since March 6. Cornelius to W. H. Fauntleroy, Camp Palluse Falls, March 22, 1856, in "Reg. Order Book," *WaSp*.

181. Lt. Richard Caldwell was ordered to "procede by water to the Encampment of Lieutenant Pillow at or near Fort Walla Walla and there obtain and make arrangements for the transportation of subsistence for five hundred men for fifteen days to the mouth of the Yackima river." Cornelius to Caldwell, Camp Collumbia river, March 29, 1856, in *ibid., WaSp*.

182. Co. A, Recruiting Battalion, Capt. E. J. Harding, cmdg., was one of the recently mutinous companies.

183. This final march through the enemy's country was initiated a few days before with the order that "All men belonging to Co. A and D, E of the 1st Batalion and B and C of Batalion of Recruits with property belonging to the same and all of the serviceable horses and cattle fit for beef you will immediately cross over the Collumbia River at Fort Walla Walla and proceede with the same to my camp at or near the mouth of the Yackima river...." Special Order, Camp Mouth Yackima, March 31, 1856, in *ibid., WaSp*. It is noteworthy that none of the recently mutinous units were included in this closing campaign.

184. Co. B, Recruiting Battalion, Capt. Benjamin Burch, cmdg., Jan. 25-May 8, 1856; Co. C, Recruiting Battalion, Capt. A. P. Ankeny, cmdg., Jan. 29-May 15, 1856.

185. It was at this camp that Capt. A. P. Ankeny added a postscript to an earlier letter with the news that "The men are much reduced by walking and driving their poor horses before them, and this night [April 12] they go to bed supperless and remain so for the next twenty-four hours before relief can reach them." A. P. Ankeny to T. J. Dryer, Camp Canyon Creek, April 10, 1856, in *Weekly Oregonian*, April 19, 1856, p. 2.

186. The troops were torn by rumors of an early discharge, or renewed campaigning in the Yakima country, or even a return to the Walla Walla Valley. What they probably did not know was the matching absence of certain knowledge plaguing their commanding colonel! He told his wife that if the governor "will give me a discharge I will come home as soon as I can get the business settled up that is concerning the redgtment so you

may rest asshured that I will bee at home in ten or twelve days from this time any way. If I can't get off any other way I will resign and come any how." Cornelius to his wife, Dalles, O.T., April 14, 1856, *CSmH*; Five days later, after complaining about the lack of definite information from Curry, Cornelius informed his wife "that I will come down tomorrow and I will make the governor a tender of my resignation and if he will except [accept] I will come home and let him fight his own Indians and if not I will return and tuff it out." T. R. Cornelius to Mrs. Florentine Cornelius, Dalles of Collumbia, April 19, 1856. Ms. *WaSp*.

# Biographical sketches

This attempt to identify every person in the text or cited in a note stems from a personal annoyance with writers who move on blithely without trying to reduce to people the names mentioned in their narratives. The uneven quality of these sketches of prominent, obscure, and transient men bears witness to the great diversity and caliber of the sources used. A few of those named withstood all efforts to pierce further into their basic anonymity. These successful defenders against every endeavor to compose a more specific identification have deprived themselves of a place among the biographical sketches, and are marked with an asterisk when their names appear in the notes.

The sources for these biographical sketches and the factual data they contain have been incorporated in the biographical section of the Vertical File in the Oregon Historical Society Library. The author cherishes the hope that all biographical corrections and additions may be sent to that permanent research resource by readers and future students.

**GEORGE ABERNETHY (1807-1877)** was born in New York City, came to Oregon, June 1, 1840, as steward of the Methodist Mission; and was made governor under the Provisional Government of Oregon, 1845-1849. He played a very important position on the Oregon business stage from 1846, when he acquired the assets of the Methodist Mission at Willamette Falls, until his ventures in milling, lumber, wholesale merchandising, ocean and river transportation failed in 1861. He continued on in Portland as a commission merchant until his death, May 2, 1877.

**J. C. AINSWORTH (1822-1893)** was born in Springborough, Ohio, reached Oregon in 1850 where he was identified with the river boat business. He was a prime mover in the formation of the Oregon Steam Navigation Company, 1860, as well as its president and very effective manager for most of its existence. He helped establish the Dalles Railroad Co., 1862; was involved in several gold and silver mining ventures, 1864, and exerted great influence in Tacoma's designation as western terminus of the Northern Pacific Railway, 1873. The sale of the Oregon Steam Navigation Company to Henry Villard in 1879 for $5,000,000 cleared the way for Ainsworth's move to California where he died, Dec. 30, 1893, near Oakland.

**BEVERELY S. ALLEN (c. 1818-1877)** was born in Carolina, admitted to the bar in Carroll County in 1840, and served twice in the Tennessee House of Representatives, 1847-1848 and 1849-1850. He was appointed special commissioner for Indian treaties in 1850 and began his brief stay in Oregon, Feb. 1851. He returned to Tennessee where he married Mary E. Doherty in 1856 and became prominent as a lawyer in Huntingdon until his death, Aug. 23, 1877.

**ALEXANDER P. ANKENY (1822-1891)** was born in Westmoreland County, Pennsylvania, reached Oregon in 1850 and farmed in Yamhill County for seven years. He served as Captain, Co. C., Recruiting Battalion, OMV, Jan.-May, 1856; and in post-war years was identified with shipping and transportation enterprises on the Columbia and Willamette rivers. He helped found the First National Bank of Portland, 1865, and the Oregon Fire and Marine Insurance Co., 1867; but in later years he was involved in the mining industry by his purchase of the Sterling mines in southern Oregon. He died at Salem, March 21, 1891.

**JAMES J. ARCHER (1817-1864)** was born at Stafford, Maryland, educated at Princeton and Bacon College, Georgetown, Kentucky. He resumed his legal practice after the Mexican War, 1848: and returned to the Army as a captain in the Ninth Infantry, March 28, 1855. He served under Col. George Wright during the spring and summer, 1856, while the U.S. Army tried to corner a sufficient number of Yakima Indians for a decent battle; Archer was, then, assigned to Ft. Simcoe in the Yakima country until its closing, May 22, 1859: when he assumed command of the escort for the Northwest Boundary Commission for the months preceding his resignation from the Army, July, 1861. He was commissioned a brigadier-general in the Army of the Confederate States, June 3,

1862, and fought in Robert E. Lee's Army of Northern Virginia until captured at Gettysburg, July 1-3, 1863. He was exchanged after more than a year in prison, resumed his former command, but deteriorating health brought death, Oct. 24, 1864.

**WILLIAM BAILEY (1829-1903)** was born in Paoli, Indiana, and came to Oregon from Iowa, 1855. After his discharge from Co. A, Multnomah County, First Regiment, OMV, in 1856, he worked as a carpenter and joiner in Walla Walla, W.T. until his return to Benton County, Oregon, in 1865. He moved to Linn County, near Creswell, in 1870: and remained there until his death, April 4, 1903.

**DAVID W. BALLARD (1824-1893)** was born in Bridgeport, Indiana, studied at Cincinnati Medical College, practiced medicine in Moravia, Indiana, before establishing himself near Lebanon, Ore., in 1852. He was one of the incorporators of the South Santiam Bridge Co., in 1857. He was a state senator from Linn County in 1862, 1864, and 1865: and after a stormy, but competent, term as governor of Idaho Territory 1866-1870 he returned to Linn County to resume the large medical practice that busied him until his death, Sept. 18, 1893.

**FRANCIS BALTIMORE (1834-1857)** emigrated to Oregon from Arkansas in 1853 to join his mother and sister in Salem. He and his brother, Noel, served in Co. A, Multnomah County, First Regiment, OMV, Oct. 1855-May, 1856. Less than a year later, Feb. 25, 1857, Francis died in Portland; and Noel died in Salem, March 12, whither he had gone to tell his mother, sister and brother of Francis' death.

**SAMUEL K. BARLOW (1795-1867)** was born in Kentucky, arrived in Oregon, 1845, where he and Philip Foster were granted a charter by the territorial legislature to build and operate a toll road. They cut a rough roadway along the south slope of Mt. Hood from Wamic to Sandy in 1846. This difficult but feasible approach ot the Willamette Valley was never especially lucrative despite initial charges of $5 per wagon (reduced to $2.50 in 1860) and 10¢ a head for loose stock. Barlow died at Canemah, the transfer point for the portage around Willamette Falls, on July 14, 1867.

**ELI M. BARNUM (1824-1881)** was born in Florence, Ohio, arrived in Oregon, June 7, 1851, and filed on a donation claim, Feb. 1, 1854. His position as Adjutant General of the Oregon Mounted Volunteers, 1855-1856, did not prevent his helping to organize the Pacific Telegraph Co., 1855: or his being a director of the Willamette Woolen Manufacturing Co., 1856. He served briefly as general agent for the new woolen industry in 1858 but may have been distracted by his unsuccessful campaign for the governorship on the Democratic ticket. He was an Oregon delegate to the 1866 National Union Convention in Philadelphia. This closed his fifteen years in Oregon for he moved to New York in 1867. Five years later he was president of the Utah Constitutional Convention, Feb. 19-March 2, 1872, and lived on as a prominent Salt Lake City attorney until his death, Sept. 23, 1881.

**CHARLES BENNETT (1811-1855)** reached Oregon from Kansas in 1844. California attracted him in 1847 where, it is claimed, he identified the gold at Sutter's Mill rather than James Marshall. After returning to Oregon, he operated Bennett House, Salem's famous hostelry, was a partner in the Willamette River steamboat, *Canemah* (built by A. F. Hedges in 1851), and was contractor for the foundations of the first Capitol building in 1854. He was Captain, Co. F, Marion County, First Regiment, OMV, from Oct. 19 until his death in the Battle of Walla Walla, Dec. 7, 1855.

**JAMES BIRNIE (c. 1799-1864)** was born in Aberdeen, Scotland, came to the Pacific coast in 1818 as a clerk for the North West Co. He was assigned to Ft. George (at the mouth of the Columbia River) 1820-1821: and after the merger of the North West Co., with the Hudson's Bay Co., in 1821, he worked at Spokane House, 1822-1823, Ft. Okanogan, 1824-1825, established a post at The Dalles, 1829, was sent to Ft. Simpson in New Caledonia, 1834-1837, and was at Ft. George 1839-1846. After retiring in this latter year he moved across the river to Cathlamet, W.T. where he was in charge of an HBC agency during the 1850s. He died Dec. 21, 1864.

**DAVID BLAINE (1824-1900)** was born in Varick, N.Y., completed his college and seminary training for the Methodist Episcopal ministry before emigrating to Seattle, W.T. Nov. 26, 1853. Mr. Blaine worked diligently in Seattle's pioneer Methodist Church prior to moving to Portland in the spring of 1856. He and his family lived and worked in different Oregon cities up to 1863, when they returned to New York for twenty years. They came back to Seattle in 1882 and remained among old friends until his death, November 26, 1900.

**AUGUSTIN MAGLIORE ALEXANDRE BLANCHET (1797-1887)**
Roman Catholic bishop, born at St. Pierre de la Riviere du Sud,
P.Q., studied at the seminary in Quebec City and was ordained a
priest, July 3, 1821. He was consecrated bishop, Sept. 27, 1846, and
came over the Oregon Trail to Walla Walla the following spring.
The Bishop of Walla Walla was transferred to the new Diocese of
Nisqually, May 31, 1850, where he remained until retiring in 1879,
eight years prior to his death, Feb. 25, 1887.

**FRANCIS NORBERT BLANCHET (1795-1883)** Roman Catholic archbishop of Oregon City, was born at St. Pierre de la Riviere du
Sud, P.Q., Sept. 3, 1795. He was ordained a priest in 1819, served a
year at the Cathedral in Quebec City, before spending seven arduous years as missionary to the Acadians and Micmac Indians of
New Brunswick. He and Abbe Modeste Demers came to Ft. Vancouver in 1838 to minister to the French and half breeds in the
Willamette Valley and Vancouver. He was consecrated bishop in
1843, and became archbishop of Oregon City three years later.
Blanchet ranged over his immense diocese working with Indian
and white while building churches, schools, and hospitals. He went
to Europe in 1846 and to South America in 1855 in search of money
and personnel for his remote jurisdiction. Worn by long years of
travel and labor he obtained Charles Seghers as his coadjutor bishop in 1879. Two years later, Blanchet resigned and lived in retirement at Providence Hospital, Portland, Oregon, until his death on
June 18, 1883.

**ANDREW J. BOLON (c. 1822-1855)** was born in Pennsylvania, emigrated to Washington Territory where he was a member of the first
territorial legislature, 1854. He was appointed Indian sub-agent
Aug. 19, 1854, for the tribes between the Bitterroot and Cascade
Mountains. His tireless travels and conferences with the interior
tribes, in the judgment of some, made him the best informed territorial official on Indian affairs east of the Cascade Mountains. He
was murdered by four Yakimas, Sept. 25, 1855.

**GEORGE C. BOMFORD (1807-1859)** was born in New York, lived in
Washington, D.C. prior to his arrival in Oregon, May, 1850. He, with
Brooke and John Noble, began cattle ranching in the Walla Walla
Valley March, 1853. His own 320 acre donation claim on the Tou-
chet River he worked from June to November, 1855, only to see it

ravished in that year's Indian fighting. His election as one of the commissioners, July 9, 1855, of recently established Walla Walla County was rendered meaningless by the war. Unlike his partners, Bomford left for Europe and died in Italy, Dec. 15, 1859.

**JOHN BAPTISTE BOULET (1834-1919)** Roman Catholic priest was born in Marieville, P.Q. He began classical studies in Pittsburgh, Pa., 1859, and his philosophy classes at St. Hyacinth Seminary, P.Q., 1863-1864 before reaching Vancouver, W.T., Oct., 1864. Here he taught in Holy Angels College for four years; then, joined Fr. Louis St. Onge at the Yakima mission, St. Joseph's on the Ahtanum where he remained until 1871. After Bishop A.M.A. Blanchet ordained him to the priesthood, July 19, 1874, Boulet spent his long, active priestly life among Indians and whites on the West side of the Cascades. He worked in Clarke, Lewis, and Skamania counties up to 1878. There followed stints of varying time spans among the Tulalip and Lummi Indians, in Ferndale, Bellingham, and other places where he built churches, schools, residences as part of his ceaseless work for people. Through all these years his interest in native languages, typesetting, and printing never flagged until his death at Bellingham, Aug. 4, 1919.

**JESSE T. BOWLES (1830-1906)** was born in Jefferson County, Mo., went to California in 1849 and settled in Oregon after a return visit to Missouri in 1852 and took a donation claim, Washington County, 1853. His service in Co. A, First Regiment, OMV, extended from Oct. 13, 1855 to May 5, 1856: followed by his enlistment in Co. B, Oregon Mounted Rangers, May 15-Aug. 21, 1856. After the Yakima War, he lived in Washington Territory for several years, even serving in the territorial legislature, 1861-1864. He returned to Oregon where he spent many years as a fruitgrower and investor until his death at Portland, June 20, 1906.

**ALLAN C. BRELSFORD (1832-1873)** was, along with John Ewry, a pioneer undertaker in Portland. He and J. T. Kern had visited the Colville mines, Sept. 1855; but returned in time to join Co. A, First Regiment, OMV, Oct. 13, 1855-May 5, 1856. He resumed his professional activities following the war. His wife divorced him Dec. 1, 1873; he left for San Francisco aboard the *Oriflamme* on Dec. 19, and disappeared from her deck off Cape Mendocino prior to her arrival in San Francisco, Christmas Day 1873.

**LLOYD BROOKE (1819-1893)** was born in Georgetown, D.C., and was a civilian employee of the U.S. Army for much of his adult life. He was in the Seminole War, 1836-1842, before coming to Ft. Vancouver as a highly-prized clerk in the quartermaster department, 1849. He joined George C. Bomford and John F. Noble in a farming and cattle-raising venture on Whitman's old mission claim, 1853, and on the Touchet River where each filed on 320 acres. He was elected Treasurer, Auditor and Probate Judge of Walla Walla County, July 9, 1855. These first sprouts of civil government were, of course, completely wilted in the Indian outburst of that year. He resumed his clerkship at Ft. Vancouver after his marriage to Genevieve Hamilton, Dec. 30, 1855. A marked change in his position became apparent nearly ten years later, 1864, by his association with J. C. Ainsworth, R. R. Thompson, and other prominent Oregon investors in the incorporation of the Empire Gold and Silver Mining Co., the Crane and Driggs Gold and Silver Mining Co., and the Morning Star Gold and Silver Mining Co. He was identified for the next 30 years, in one way or other, with the Quartermaster Department as civilian clerk, agent, or transportation agent in Portland. His name was linked with various financial schemes as his own resources and stature grew, and he never lost his zest for turning a profit to the day he died, May 29, 1893.

**WILLIAM S. BUCKLEY (1829-1891)** was born in West Virginia, came to Oregon in Oct., 1852, and settled a donation claim in Clackamas County, 1853. He served in Co. I, First Regiment, OMV, Oct. 31, 1855-Feb. 2, 1856: in Co. A, Feb. 2, 1856-March 20, 1856; and as Captain, Co. K, Oregon Mounted Rangers, April 3, 1856-June 23, 1856. He stayed in Portland for four years after the war; thence, moved to Stockton, California where he lived for more than 30 years until his death, April 2, 1891.

**BENJAMIN F. BURCH (1825-1893)** was born near Keytesville, Missouri, emigrated to Oregon in 1845, fought the Cayuse Indians in 1848, and settled on a donation claim near Independence, Oregon, 1849. After serving in the Yakima War, 1855-56, he held a number of appointive and elective offices in the state. He was a member of the State Constitutional Convention, 1857: a member of the 1858 Legislature, of the Senate in 1858, President of the Senate in 1870: Superintendent of the Penitentiary, 1877, and Receiver of the Oregon Land Office in 1887. He died in his Independence home, March 24, 1893.

140

**ASAHEL BUSH (1824-1913)** came to Oregon in 1850, after his admission to the Massachusetts bar, in time to serve as clerk of the Territorial lower house, 1850-1851. He began publishing the *Oregon Statesman* in Oregon City, March, 1851, but moved it to Salem two years later. His long tenure as public printer, 1851-1864, reflected his influence in Democratic Party circles as did his membership in the powerful Salem Clique along with L. F. Glover, B. F. Harding, R. B. Boise, J. W. Nesmith, George L. Curry and others. The Ladd and Bush Bank, a partnership with William S. Ladd, opened in Salem, 1868. He retained his forceful voice in Oregon affairs until his death at Salem, Dec. 23, 1913.

**ANDREW J. CAIN (c. 1829-1879)** was born in Indiana, came to Washington Territory in 1853 with Isaac I. Stevens' railroad survey party, was appointed Indian Agent for the tribes along the north bank of the Columbia River, 1855-1857, and for those in the Walla Walla district, 1859-1861. He was a major real estate promoter in Walla Walla, 1861-1866; practiced law and was prosecuting attorney there, 1869, and county auditor in 1875. He began publishing the *Dayton News,* Sept. 1874, and at one time or other was associated with the *Umatilla Press* and the *Walla Walla Real Estate Gazette.* Death ended his energetic life, July 6, 1879.

**RICHARD S. CALDWELL (1830-1869)** born in Massachusetts, was working as a clerk in Washington County, Oregon by 1850. He enlisted in Co. D, Washington County, and served as a private, Oct. 17, 1855-Jan. 28, 1856: and as a lieutenant, Jan. 29-May 15, 1856. He was an accountant after the war for Allen and Lewis, a Portland wholesale supply firm. He died in Providence, R.I., March 17, 1869, while visiting his brother, Rev. Samuel L. Caldwell, prominent local clergyman.

**JAMES M. CAMPBELL (1833-1922)** was born in Morgan County, Illinois: lived in Iowa, 1842-1853, and came with his parents to Oregon in the latter year. He prospected in the Yreka gold field and herded cattle before enlisting in Co. G, Polk County, First Regiment, OMV, Capt. Benjamin Hayden, cmdg. (after the election of Capt. A. N. Armstrong as major of the regiment, Oct. 30, 1855). After the Yakima War he looked for work in the Idaho gold boom town of Florence, 1862. He finally settled in Dallas, Oregon, where he lived a long life as carpenter, merchant and mortician until his own death, 1922.

**WILLIAM A. CASON (1828-1865)** was born in Virginia, reached Oregon in 1843 where he settled on a donation claim in March, 1851. Against the Yakima Indians he served briefly in Co. G, Polk County, First Regiment, OMV, until his transfer to Co. C, Clackamas County, Oct. 31, 1855. He was elected captain of Co. E, Recruiting Battalion, Feb. 22-June 10, 1856. He was still a young man nine years after the war when his body was found on the road a half mile from his home, Dec. 3, 1865.

**W. W. CHAPMAN (1808-1892)** was born in Virginia, appointed U.S. Attorney for Wisconsin Territory in 1836: and elected territorial delegate from Iowa, 1838. He was in Oregon for a brief stay in 1847, moved on to California the next year, and was back in Oregon in time for election to the 1849 Territorial Legislature: later, 1858, 1859, he was elected to the State Legislature. His business interests were diversified with his one-third interest in the Portland townsite purchased from Daniel Lownsdale and Stephen Coffin in 1849, and his acquisition of the Ft. Umpqua assets of the Hudson's Bay Co. in 1853. This latter transaction gave him a personal motive for his service against the Rogue River Indians 1855-56. He moved to Corvallis in 1856 where he stayed a year until his appointment as surveyor general of Oregon took him to Eugene. Portland and the practice of law attracted him from 1861 to the end of his life, Oct. 18, 1892.

**HENRY M. CHASE (1831-1899)** was born in Philadelphia, Pa., came to the Umatilla area with Wm. McKay toward the end of 1851, and ran a cattle ranch on the Touchet River (near present Dayton, Washington) until 1855. He lived in Walla Walla until after 1882, and moved to Barnstable, Mass. for the years preceding his death in Boston, Nov. 18, 1899.

**MARK A. CHINN (1823-1856)** was born in Kentucky, filled a prime role in the attempted organization of the Whig Party in Oregon, 1854. He served in Co. E, First Regiment, OMV, Oct. 15-Oct. 30, 1855; then, as junior Major of the Regiment until the Volunteers were disbanded. He traveled to the Sandwich Islands, May, 1856, in a futile effort to recover from tuberculosis. The day after returning from the Islands, June 17, 1856, he died in San Francisco.

**EUGENE CASIMIR CHIROUSE (c. 1820-1892)** Roman Catholic priest, born at Bourg du Peage, near Valence, France, joined the

Oblates of Mary Immaculate, and came to Ft. Walla Walla where he was ordained a priest by Bishop A.M.A. Blanchet, Jan. 2, 1848. He was stationed among the Cayuse and Yakima tribes until the fighting began in 1855. Later he spent many years among the Snohomish Indians at Tulalip; then with the natives on Vancouver Island and the lower Fraser River. He retired to New Westminster, B.C., where he died, May 28, 1892.

**STEPHEN COFFIN (1807-1882)** was born in Maine, came to Oregon City in 1847, but quickly committed his assets by buying a half interest in the Portland townsite from A. L. Lovejoy and Francis Pettygrove, 1849. He was the prime mover in building the Tualatin Plank Road, 1851: important in the founding of the People's Trans-poration Co., for freight and passengers on the Willamette River, 1860; a major stockholder in the Oregon Iron Works at Oswego, and builder of a large sawmill in eastern Oregon, 1862. This powerful figure in Oregon development died March 15, 1882.

**SAMUEL COOPER (   ?-1876)** was born in New York, appointed to West Point from his native state, May 25, 1813, and followed the customary route of military advancement to the rank of Colonel, July 15, 1852. Nine years later he resigned his commission, March 7, 1861, to accept the position of Adjutant General and Inspector General in the Army of the Confederate States of America until the end of the Civil War. He died on Dec. 3, 1876.

**THOMAS R. CORNELIUS (1827-1899)** was born in Missouri, came to Oregon in 1845, fought in the Cayuse War of 1848 before looking for California gold, only to return to Oregon where he settled on a Washington County donation claim, 1850. He was Captain of Co. D, First Regiment, OMV, Oct. 15-Dec. 21, 1855; then Colonel of the Regiment, after James Nesmith's resignation, until the campaign's finish, May, 1856. Later, 1861-1862, he was Colonel in the Oregon Cavalry. He was, throughout life, prominent in politics, being elected to the Territorial Council in 1856, 1857 and 1858; to the State Senate, 1859, 1860, 1865, 1866, 1868, 1870, 1872 and 1874. He was defeated as Republican candidate for Governor in 1886. He estab-lished the town of Cornelius in 1872, and here he owned a store, sawmill, warehouse and nearby farm. Here, too, he died, June 24, 1899.

**NARCISSE A. CORNOYER (1820-1909)** was born in Illinois, worked for the American Fur Company in the Rocky Mountains in the 1840s, looked for gold in California, 1849, and settled on his Marion County donation claim, 1851. He fought in the Rogue River War, 1853, and against the Yakimas he was Captain, Co. K, First Regiment, OMV, Oct. 30, 1855-March 7, 1856. The unusual services of this select company were partially recognized by his election as 1st Major of the Regiment, March 7, 1856. Upon his return to Marion County he was twice elected Sheriff beginning in 1856. Three years, c. 1860-1863, were spent in an unsuccessful quartz mining venture in eastern Oregon. The remainder of his long life was linked with this portion of the state. He was superintendent of farming at the Umatilla Agency, c. 1869-1871, Indian Agent of the Umatillas, 1871-1875, and again, 1876-1880. The Indians gave him 160 acres which he farmed until he died, March 31, 1909.

**JOHN E. W. COTTINGHAM (1826-1915)** was born in Snowhill, Maryland, was living in Benton County, Oregon by 1854, and served in Co. I, Benton County, First Regiment, OMV, Oct. 20, 1855-Feb. 2, 1856. He lived most of his long active life as a carpenter at The Dalles: his closing years were spent at the Veterans' Home at Roseburg, Ore., where he died, Oct. 21, 1915.

**WILLIAM COWAN (1818-1902)** another Hudson's Bay Co. man came to York Factory (at the mouth of Nelson River on the west shore of Hudson Bay) in 1848. He was stationed at the Red River Settlement (along the banks of the Red River and Assiniboine River at their juncture), 1849-1856: then, at Moose Factory (at the mouth of the Moose River on the southwest shore of James' Bay), 1856-1863. He spent 1863 at Ft. Garry in the Red River Settlement, took his children to London for schooling in 1864, and came back to Ft. Garry the next year. He was placed in charge of the Fort in 1867, three years before being imprisoned by Louis Riel, the *metis* leader. A two year sojourn in London followed his escape from detention; whence he returned to Ft. Garry to remain until his death in 1902.

**WILLIAM CRAIG (1807-1869)** was born in Virginia, came to the Rocky Mountain region in 1829, and ranged over the West with different fur outfits until he began farming in Nez Perce country in 1840. He filed on a piece of land farther up Lapwai Creek, 1846, after Henry Spalding insisted that Craig's first farm was on land needed by the mission. By reason of his wife, Isabel, being the daughter of

Chief James of the Nez Perce, Craig was an effective liaison man in 1848 after the Whitman Massacre of Nov. 1847; and as interpreter, guide, and go-between for Governor Isaac Stevens' councils of 1855 at Walla Walla, Hellgate, and with the Blackfoot. He recruited and commanded a company of Nez Perce volunteers in the Washington Territorial Volunteers, 1855-1856. He was Indian sub-agent at Walla Walla, 1857: where he was postmaster, 1858-59, and ferry operator on the Clearwater River at Spalding, Idaho, 1861-1864. He had a paralytic stroke in 1869 and died in September of that year.

**JAMES CURL (1798-1863)** was born in Montgomery County, Kentucky, traveled over the Oregon Trail to Linn County, Oregon, Oct. 1847. He was commissioned County Probate Judge, 1850: elected representative to the Territorial Legislature, 1852-1853, and during the Yakima War served in Co. D, Recruiting Battalion, Feb. 1-May 26, 1856. He died at Scio, Linn County, Jan. 7, 1863.

**GEORGE LAW CURRY (1820-1878)** was born in Pennsylvania, was a newspaper publisher in St. Louis prior to emigrating to Oregon City, 1846, where he edited the *Oregon Spectator* for a year, and founded the *Free Press,* 1848. He was elected to Oregon's Provisional Legislature, 1848-1849, was Chief Clerk of the Legislative Council, 1850-1852, Secretary of the Provisional Government, 1853: Acting Governor in 1853 and again in 1854: finally becoming Governor, Nov. 1, 1854-March 3, 1859. He returned to journalism as editor of the (Portland) *Daily Advertiser,* 1861-1862; and later of the (Portland) *Evening Journal,* 1876. He died two years later, July 28, 1878.

**ANSON DART (1797-1879)** was born in Vermont, moved to Montrose, Pa. in 1816, later speculated profitably in wheat and land near Utica, N.Y., prior to sustaining staggering losses in Wisconsin timber and real estate in the depressed market following 1837. He spent ten years, 1840-1850, as developer and promoter of the area near Green Lake, Wis. His two years, 1850-1852, as Superintendent of Indian Affairs for Oregon, were prelude for the next thirty he lived in New York and Washington, D.C., mostly in minor government positions until his death in 1879.

**JOHN WYNN DAVIDSON (1823-1881)** was born in Virginia and was appointed to West Point, July 1, 1841. His military career followed the familiar path of 2nd Lieutenant, First Dragoons, July 1, 1845, and promotion to Captain on Jan. 15, 1855, a few months before his tour at Ft. Vancouver. His Civil War service was recognized shortly before Robert E. Lee's surrender at Appomattox Courthouse, April 9, 1865, by his promotion to Brigadier General in the Volunteers and in the U.S. Regular Army (Bvt.). He was raised to full Colonel in the Regular Army March 20, 1879, slightly more than two years before his death, June 26, 1881, in St. Paul, Minn.

**EDWARD HENRY DAY (    ?-1860)** was born in Virginia, appointed to West Point from Tennessee, July 1, 1847, and brevetted a 2nd Lieutenant, July 1, 1851. He was promoted to 1st Lieutenant, March 3, 1855, a few months prior to the outbreak of the Yakima War. About 1856 he took sick leave and returned East where he died, Jan. 2, 1860.

**AUGUSTIN DeLORE (1818-    ?)** farmed on French Prairie with the sizable group of retired French Canadian HBC employees. He lived at Oak Grove, Oregon after 1856.

**MODESTE DEMERS (1809-1871),** born Oct. 11, 1809 in St. Nicholas, P.Q., completed his seminary studies in Quebec City where he was ordained a priest, Feb. 7, 1836. Two years later he and Rev. Francis N. Blanchet came to the Oregon Country. Demers spent nine diligent years among the natives and the few whites north of the Columbia River, in New Caledonia, and Alaska before his consecration as first bishop of Vancouver Island, Nov. 30, 1847. He remained as spiritual guide to his people until a paralytic stroke, New Year's Day, 1871, presaged his death months later at Victoria, B.C., July 28, 1871.

**AMMI PRINCE DENNISON (1827-1896)** was born in Freeport, Maine, and came to Oregon by ship in 1850. He was elected to the Portland City Council in 1852 and 1855: and was President of the State Senate, 1855, 1856. He was Gov. George Curry's aide-de-camp throughout the Yakima War: then, Indian Agent on the Warm Springs Reservation, 1858-60, a delegate to the 1860 Democratic National Convention: and recruiting officer and quartermaster at Ft. Dalles, 1861. His several years as director of Multnomah County School District No. 1 ended about 1871 with his departure for San Francisco where he worked in the U.S. Mint, and died, June 5, 1896.

146

**JAMES DOTY, JR. (1827-1857)** was born near Green Bay, Wis., but moved to Madison in 1841 during his father's first term as Governor of Wisconsin Territory. This very talented young man joined Isaac Stevens' survey party in 1853 and was assigned to Ft. Benton, on the upper Missouri River, 1853-1854, to make meteorological observations, take a census of the Blackfoot Indians, and cultivate the neighboring tribes. Once arrived in Washington Territory, he served Stevens as secretary, aide, and liaison man in preparing the way for several important councils. The precise and detailed records of Stevens' meetings with the various tribes were Doty's work. Death came by his own hand, June 26, 1857.

**BENJAMIN F. DOWELL (1826-1897)** was born in Virginia, practiced law in Tennessee for two years before emigrating to Oregon via California in 1850. He centered his freighting and trading activities in southern Oregon, 1852-1856. The Quartermaster General OMV, employed him as Packmaster for the First Regiment, OMV, in the Yakima War. These outside interests were always in addition to his law practice in Jacksonville, Oregon, 1857-1885. His final years before death in 1897 were divided between Portland and Washington, D.C.

**JOSEPH W. DREW (    ?-1883)** was a member of the Klamath Exploring Expedition in 1850, and joined with Dr. E. P. Drew in purchasing the site of Umpqua City, 1851. He was elected to the Territorial Legislature from Umpqua County, June 1851, selected as one of the road commissioners the next year, and appointed Deputy U.S. Marshal in 1853. He was defeated in his run for the U.S. Senate in 1860 but won election as a State Senator two years later. He was an Army paymaster, 1864-1869, and was prominent in southern Oregon until his death, April 25, 1883.

**THOMAS J. DRYER (1808-1879)** was born in western New York, and divided his adult years between Ohio and New York until moving to California, 1848-1849. There Wm. W. Chapman and Stephen Coffin prevailed upon him to establish a newspaper in Portland. The first issue of the *Weekly Oregonian* appeared Dec. 4, 1850. When the Oregon Mounted Volunteers took the field against the Indians, 1855-1856, Dryer arranged with several of the fighters to send him letters during the campaign. Some of these mounted reporters signed their names while others, like "Jon" and "Wasco" preserved their anonymity. Dryer was a better journalist than business manager. The typesetter, Henry L. Pittock, hired by Dryer in 1853, had financial control of the paper for unpaid wages by 1860. The *Weekly Oregonian* came under Pittock's complete control, Jan. 12, 1861. Fiscal worries, however, were no bridle on Dryer's political career. He was in the Territorial Legislature, 1856-1859, and a member of the Oregon Constitutional Convention, 1857. President Abraham Lincoln appointed him U.S. Minister to the Sandwich Islands, 1861-1865. Upon his return to Portland, c. 1865, he was a justice of the peace for several years before his death in Salt Lake City, March 30, 1879.

**THEODORE JOHN ECKERSON (1821-1906)** was born in New York City, joined the U.S. Army in time to fight in the Seminole War, 1840-1842, and the Mexican War, 1846-1848. He was assigned to Ft. Vancouver, May 15, 1849, where he was commissioned a Lieutenant, Sept. 1853. He endeared himself to the people of Oregon and Washington territories by honoring requisitions for arms and supplies issued by Gov. George Curry of Oregon and Acting-Gov. Chas. Mason of Washington in Oct. 1855. Lt. John Withers refused to issue U.S. property but Eckerson acted without orders from Washington and despite Gen. John E. Wool's remonstrances because of the critical situation prevailing in both territories. Eckerson continued in the Army for 30 more years that saw his promotion to Captain, 1865: Major in 1881, and his retirement, 1885. He lived in Portland until his death, Apr. 4, 1906.

**WILLIAM H. FARRAR (1826-1873)** was born in New Hampshire and came to Oregon in 1853 when appointed territorial District Attorney. He served as Adjutant, First Regiment, OMV, throughout the Yakima War; was a delegate to the Oregon Constitutional Convention, 1857; was Mayor of Portland, 1862-1863, and a member of the Oregon delegation to the National Union Party Convention in Philadelphia, Aug. 14, 1866. He practiced law in Washington, D.C. for the next seven years until his death, Nov. 21, 1873.

**WILLIAM HALE FAUNTLEROY (1824-1909)** was born in Virginia, resigned from the U.S. Navy in 1848, yet filled a steady role in maritime affairs from California to Washington. He served in varying positions aboard many Pacific Coast ships, 1849-1876. He was Captain of the *Multnomah,* 1852-1853: served under James Alden surveying Pacific Coast harbors aboard the *Active,* 1853, and commanded the *America, Sea Bird,* and *Goliah* in the coastal trade during 1854. While visiting in The Dalles, the Yakima War erupted, 1855, and Governor Curry appointed Fauntleroy Quartermaster and Commissary, First Regiment, OMV. He filled the post, despite some criticism of his efficiency, from Nov. 7, 1855 to June 28, 1856. Upon his return to California, he commanded different ships, surveyed Humboldt Bay and adjoining county lines in northern California, 1861-1875, and participated in surveys and real estate promotions in Santa Barbara and Kern counties, California, 1881-1901. He died at Soldier's Home, California, July 30, 1909.

**EZRA T. T. FISHER (1835-1899)** was born in Indianapolis and came to Oregon when ten years of age. He was Acting Quartermaster and Commissary, First Regiment, OMV, March 1-May 15, 1856, i.e., until Col. James Kelly's command returned to Ft. Henrietta. He was a State Representative from Clackamas County, 1864-65; and much later, County Surveyor, 1884 until his death on his large farm near Albany, Oregon, Feb. 11, 1899.

**JESSE FLEMING (1811-1855)** was born in North Carolina, settled on his donation claim, Multnomah County, Dec. 1, 1850. He served in Co. A, Multnomah County, First Regiment, OMV, Oct. 13, 1855 until he died, Dec. 13, as a result of wounds received during the Battle of Walla Walla, Dec. 8, 1855.

**JACOB FRITZ (1828-1898)** was born in Nassau, Nuderzingheim, Germany and brought to the U.S. when 16 years old. Here he served in the U.S. Army, 1849-1861: then in the Oregon Volunteers until 1865, and as a civilian employee of the U.S. Army until 1875. There followed a long association with the Oregon Steam Navigation Co., and its successor, the Oregon Railway and Navigation Co., that ended only with his death at The Dalles, Feb. 4, 1898.

**JOHN POLLARD GAINES (1795-1857)** was born in Virginia, served as aide to General Winfield Scott in the Mexican War, 1846-1847, and was elected U.S. Representative from Kentucky, 1847-1849. President Zachary Taylor appointed him Governor of Oregon Territory in 1850. He filled this office from Aug. 18, 1850 until replaced by acting-Governor George L. Curry, May 16, 1853. A week later he settled on a donation land claim near Salem where he lived until his death on Dec. 9, 1857.

**GEORGE GIBBS (1815-1873)** was born in Sunswick, Long Island, graduated from Harvard Law School in 1838, practiced law in New York, and spent 1842-1846 as librarian of the New York Historical Society. He came to Oregon with the Mounted Rifle Regiment in 1849, and was appointed Collector of Customs at Astoria three different times: 1851, 1853, and 1858. He spent portions of 1855-1857 exploring the Umpqua region, the Cascade Mountains, and Puget Sound. His major ethnological studies were incorporated in the Pacific Railroad Survey, 1853-1855. His excursions in the Northwest were concluded by his three years on the International Boundary Survey along the forty-ninth parallel, 1857-1860. He filled various appointive offices upon his return to Washington, D.C. until his death in New Haven, Conn., Apr. 9, 1873.

**GRANVILLE O. HALLER (1819-1897)** was born in Pennsylvania, commissioned a 2nd Lt., U.S. Infantry, 1839, and twice cited for gallantry during the Mexican War. Assigned to the Department of the Pacific in 1852, he served at different times in Idaho, Oregon, Washington, Arizona and California. He served under General George McClellan from 1861 until his dismissal for "disloyal conduct" in July, 1863. It took 13 years, until 1879, for him to be completely exonerated and restored to rank. He lived near Port Townsend, Washington Territory, and farmed on Whidbey Island during these years spent in clearing his reputation. After his retirement, Feb. 6, 1882, he lived in Seattle until his death, May 2, 1897.

**ARCHIMEDES HANAN (1810-1902)** was born in Kentucky, lived in Illinois, Missouri, Iowa and Minnesota before settling near Albany, Oregon in 1852. He served in Co. H, Linn County, First Regiment, OMV, Capt. Davis Layton, cmdg., from Oct. 17, 1855-March 12, 1856. He sold his partial interest in an unprofitable Albany flouring mill in 1865; and six years later, at the age of 61, he moved to Columbia County, W.T., where he became a substantial landowner in the remaining years of his life that ended, Feb. 2, 1902.

**ADOLPHUS BRICE HANNAH (1822-1905)** was born in Illinois, lived in Iowa Territory before emigrating to Oregon in 1845. His adult life was intertwined with that of Morton M. McCarver in California, Oregon and Washington. Hannah was deputy sheriff of Clackamas County, Oregon, 1847-1848; sheriff of Sacramento, California, 1849-1850, and served in Co. C, Clackamas County, 1st Regt., OMV., as 1st Lieutenant under Captains James Kelly and Samuel Stafford (after his election Nov. 4, 1855) from Oct. 16, 1855 to Feb. 17, 1856. He was elected to the Oregon Legislature, 1858, appointed U.S. Marshal, 1860, chosen as a delegate to the Washington Constitutional Convention, 1878, and elected a member of Tacoma's City Council, 1886-1887. His business affairs were usually linked with those of McCarver. He invested his gold dust in infant Sacramento, 1849, engaged in Willamette River steamboating, 1856-1857, and was involved in the creation of Tacoma, 1868. Here he remained a prominent and influential figure until his death, June 16, 1905.

**BENJAMIN M. HARDING (c. 1828-    )** Lieutenant, Co. A, Multnomah County, First Regiment, OMV, served from Oct. 13, 1855-May 15, 1856, for a total of 216 days.

**ELISHA JENKINS HARDING (1828-1897)** was born in Pennsylvania, and arrived in Oregon about 1850 where he bought squatter rights from former Hudson's Bay Co. employees on French Prairie (near present St. Paul, Ore.): thus, eventually accumulating about 2,000 acres. He was Captain, Co. A, Recruiting Battalion, First Regiment, OMV, Jan. 24-May 19, 1856; and served again in Co. B, First Oregon Cavalry in 1861. These two military tours and one term as clerk of the U.S. District Court were the only noteworthy departures from his successful life as a farmer that closed in March, 1897.

**BENJAMIN HAYDEN (1822-1908)** was born in Kentucky, lived in Missouri and California before emigrating to Oregon in 1852. He settled on a donation claim near Eola, Polk County, 1854. He was elected Captain, Co. G, Nov. 2, 1855, after Capt. A. N. Armstrong was chosen as Major of the Regiment, Oct. 30, 1855. Hayden was elected to the State Legislature in 1857 and was Speaker of the House, 1870. His long life ended Oct. 29, 1908.

**ABSALOM FONTS HEDGES (1817-1890)** was born in McConnelsville, Ohio, came to Oregon from Iowa in 1844, and built the riverboats *Canemah* in 1851 and *Willamette,* 1853-54. He was a delegate to the State Constitutional Convention, 1857, and a member of the first legislature in 1858. He was Indian Agent for Oregon, 1853-57, and Sheriff of Clackamas County, 1872-74. He died in Yakima, Wash., March 6, 1890.

**ABSALOM J. HEMBREE (1813-1856)** was born in Tennessee, came from Missouri to Yamhill County, Oregon in 1843. He was elected

Sheriff in 1846, and a member of the Provisional Legislature, 1846, '47 and '50. He was a director of the Portland and Valley Plank Road Co., 1849, and president of the Pacific Telegraph Co., organized in 1850 to link California and Oregon. He was Captain, Co. E, Yamhill County, First Regiment, OMV, Oct. 19, 1855 until his death in a final skirmish with the Yakimas, Apr. 11, 1856.

**WAMAN CLARK HEMBREE (1829-1920)** was born in Tennessee, came to Oregon from Missouri in Nov. 1843, and settled in Yamhill County. He was constable, deputy sheriff and collector for the county at various times during a long life that ended March 22, 1920.

**JOHN P. HIBLER (1826-1874)** was born in St. Louis County, Mo., came to Oregon in 1851, and settled on his donation claim, Yamhill County, 1853. He was First Lieutenant, Co. E, Yamhill County, First Regiment, OMV, Oct. 19, 1855-May 7, 1856. He sold his land claim on March 26, 1858, returned to Missouri where he enlisted in the Missouri Rifle Battalion, First Regiment, May-Aug., 1861; and the Missouri Infantry, Twenty-ninth Battalion, Oct. 1862-Oct. 1863. He practiced dentistry after the Civil War until his death, Sept. 5, 1874.

**JAMES HILL (1832-1863)** was born in Ohio, came to Oregon in October, 1852, and settled on his donation claim in Polk County, June 1, 1854. He died in 1863.

**GEORGE H. HIMES (1844-1940)** was born in Troy, Pennsylvania, lived in Illinois, 1847-1853, when his family emigrated to a farm near Olympia, W.T. He learned the printer's trade while working on the Olympia *Standard* in 1861. After he moved to Portland in 1864 he was connected with the printing business in one guise or another for many years. He was a moving force in organizing the Oregon Pioneer Association, and became assistant secretary and curator of the Oregon Historical Society from its earliest years. He died Jan. 6, 1940.

**HENRY C. HODGES (          )** entered West Point, July 1, 1847, and was brevetted 2nd Lieutenant, 4th Infantry, exactly four years later. His nearly 50 years in the Army followed the usual course of promotions from Regimental Adjutant, 1855-1861 to Colonel, Asst. Quartermaster General, 1888, with retirement on Jan. 11, 1895.

**HARVEY A. HOGUE (1832-1902)** was born in Princeton, Indiana, traveled to California in 1850, and opened a store in Burlington, Linn County, Ore., 1852. He served in Co. H, First Regiment, OMV, Davis Layton, cmdg., 1855-56, for the most part as Quartermaster Sergeant. Twice he was chosen a member of the State House, in 1865 and 1897. His business activities were varied and successful: he sold cattle in the California and Fraser River gold fields immediately after the Yakima War; then, prospered in the lumber industry, and eventually invested in a Portland street transit system as well as in East Portland's first electric plant, 1887. He died in Winthrop, Mass., Aug. 15, 1902, but was buried in Portland.

**LOT HOLINGER (c. 1821-1856)** came to Oregon in 1850 from Philadelphia. He worked in the river trade until his death as Corporal, Co. B, First Regiment, OMV, April 23, 1856.

**MILTON HOUSTON (1830-1887)** was born in Ohio, came to Oregon in 1848 and settled on his donation claim near Albany, Linn County, Jan. 15, 1851. His Yakima War service was in Co. H, First Regiment, OMV, Capt. Davis Layton, cmdg., Oct. 17, 1855-April 7, 1856. He died on Feb. 1, 1887, still not an old man, despite the 30 post war years he had worked.

**ORLANDO HUMASON (1828-1875)** was born in Ohio and came to Oregon through Texas and California, 1849-1851. Several times he sat in the territorial and state legislatures, 1852-54, 1862, 1866; he advocated the formation of Wasco County, 1854, and helped found Dalles City, 1855, besides being county judge, 1858. Although he was Captain, Co. B, First Regiment, OMV, 1855-1856, Lt. John T. Jefferies exercised command during the fighting at Walla Walla, Dec. 1855 because of Humason's illness. His business ventures were concerned with moving people and freight. He received a license for a ferry across the Snake River, 1854. He and Robert Thompson owned the Dalles-DesChutesville Portage Freight and Passenger Co., 1857-1862. When this was merged with the Oregon Steam Navigation Co. he received 34 shares in this rewarding monopoly. He became one of six owners of the Willamette Falls and Lock Co. in 1868. Death came at his prime, Sept. 8, 1875.

**JOHN T. JEFFRIES (    ?-1867)** served in Co. B, Wasco County, First Regiment, OMV, as 1st Lieutenant, transferred to Co. G, Polk County for a short time, only to return to Co. B upon his election as

Captain, March-May, 1856. This pioneer attorney died of tuberculosis, Feb. 24, 1867.

**JACOB R. JOHN (1802-1863)** was born in Tennessee, lived in Ohio and Iowa before emigrating to Oregon in 1852. He located on the North Fork of the Lewis River several miles from Vancouver, W.T., 1853: and moved to Mill Plain, closer to the settlement, in 1861 where he stayed until death, Dec. 10, 1863.

**SAMUEL JOHNSON (1821-1907)** was born in Scioto County, Ohio, grew up in Indiana, and spent 1840-1850 in Caldwell County, Missouri, except for 1848-1849 when he was a teamster for the St. Louis Fur Company at Ash Hollow on the Platte River. He reached The Dalles in Oct., 1850, worked there in the winter, and moved on to the Yreka gold fields, in 1851. He was hired as wagon master for the Oregon Mounted Volunteers during the Yakima War and as wagon master to haul supplies for various Indian agents until 1858. He was wagon master for Humason and Thompson's Dalles-Des Chutesville Portage Freight and Passenger Co. until 1861, and was occupied in freighting from Walla Walla to the Idaho mines, 1862-1865, before finally settling on a farm on Dry Creek (just over the Oregon line) that he worked for more than 30 years prior to his death in Walla Walla, Apr. 23, 1907.

**DAVID RUMPH JONES (1825-1863)** was born in Orangesburg District, S.C., graduated from West Point in 1846, and fought in the Mexican War the following year. He was attached to the Department of the Adjutant General, 1853, and was assigned later to the Department of the Pacific; and then to St. Louis, Missouri. He resigned from the U.S. Army, Feb. 15, 1861 to start a varied and distinguished career in the Confederate Army until his death, Jan. 15, 1863.

**JACOB KAMM (1823-1912)** was born in Switzerland, worked on the Mississippi River steamboats before coming to California in 1849 where he was on the Sacramento River boats. He came to Oregon in 1850 and was ever after associated with the river borne traffic as boat owner and operator. When the Oregon Steam Navigation Co. was formed, his assets made him and R. R. Thompson the major stockholders in this transportation monopoly. After the purchase of the OSN Co., by the Henry Villard interests, Kamm kept his home in Portland until his death Dec. 14, 1912.

154

**JOSIAH P. KELLER (   ?-1862)** was born in East Machias, Maine, where he and Charles E. Foster owned a shipyard before Keller joined A. J. Pope and W. C. Talbot in various California lumber enterprises in 1849. He built and managed the sawmill owned by Pope, Talbot, Keller and Foster in 1853 at Teekalet (later, Port Gamble, Washington). He retained his interest in the Maine shipyard where he spent 1858-1861 helping to build the *Victor*. Shortly after returning to Teekalet he went to Victoria, B.C. for medical care: here he died, June 11, 1862.

**CLINTON KELLY (1808-1875)** was born in Kentucky where he lived for almost 40 years until the Methodist Episcopal Church's grave split over the matter of slavery impelled his move to Oregon, 1848. He was a devout licensed minister, and an alert land developer: positions from which he exercised considerable influence in church and civic affairs until his death, June 19, 1875.

**ELIZABETH CLARK KELLY (1843-1930)** was born near Ann Arbor, Michigan, came to Oregon in 1860, taught school and married Plympton J. Kelly, July 4, 1864. She was a devoted member of the Methodist Church in which she taught Sunday School for many years. She was a faithful supporter of the Women's Christian Temperance Union in all of her active years. She died at Portland, July 24, 1930.

**HAMPTON KELLY (1830-1898)** was born in Kentucky and came to Oregon with his father, Clinton, in 1848. He lived with his parents on their farm in Powell Valley, three miles east of Portland, until he purchased a portion of the Edward Long donation claim on which he operated a water-powered sawmill and box factory for 12 years. His chronic asthma induced him to file on a donation claim near Wapinitia, Wasco County, 1879. Here he ran a large cattle and wheat ranch, was instrumental in opening up the entire area, and continued his family's traditional devotion to the Methodist Church. He died Oct. 16, 1898.

**JAMES KERR KELLY (1819-1903)** was born in Pennsylvania where he practiced law until moving to California, 1849. He came to Oregon City in 1851, entered a legal partnership with the distinguished A. L. Lovejoy that brought rapid recognition. He assisted in compiling a legal code for Oregon, 1852-1853, and was appointed one of the Oregon Code Commissioners, 1853. He was a member of the

Oregon Legislative Council, 1853-1857, and was a delegate to the Oregon Constitutional Convention, Aug. 17-Sept. 18, 1857. His committee was charged with drafting the executive and administrative articles of the constitution. He organized and was elected Captain, Co. C, First Regiment, OMV, Oct. 16, 1855. Two weeks later, Oct. 30, he was chosen Colonel of the First Regiment and served until the Volunteers were discharged, except for his absence to attend the Legislative Council sessions. The remainder of his long life was a balance between political and professional recognition. He was a State Senator, 1860-1864: U.S. Senator, 1871-1877, and Chief Justice of the Oregon Supreme Court, 1878-1880. He lived in different cities during these years; The Dalles, 1862-1869, Portland, 1869-1890, and retired in Washington, D.C., 1890-Sept. 15, 1903.

**THOMAS KELLY (1829-1903)** was born in Kentucky and emigrated to Oregon with his brother, Clinton, 1848. He operated a sawmill until 1854 when he began farming in earnest. He served in the Yakima War, 1855-1856; and 15 years later, 1871, he moved to the Wenas area, some 12 miles northwest of Yakima City, W.T. There he built up a sizable stock ranch where he lived the rest of his life that ended, Nov. 15, 1903.

**JOHN TULLY KERN (1832-1872)** was born in Rock Creek, Ohio, emigrated to Oregon from Indiana in 1852; and was elected a member of the Oregon House of Representatives as well as a Clackamas County delegate to the 1862 Union State Convention at Eugene. The closing ten years of his life, until May 26, 1872, he served as Captain on several Willamette and Columbia River steamboats.

**WILLIAM SARGENT LADD (1826-1893)** was born in New Hampshire and came to Oregon in 1851 where he prospered from the outset. His interests mirrored the economic history of Oregon from the opening of W.S. Ladd & Co., 1852, a moderately successful mercantile store. He became an important stockholder in the Willamette Woolen Manufacturing Co., by 1856; the Ladd and Tilton Bank (with the backing of New Hampshire financier, Charles E. Tilton) opened in 1859; the Oregon Steam Navigation Co. organized in 1860; the Oregon Telegraph Co. in 1862; and the Oregon Iron and Steel Co., the Oregon Central Railroad, and the Oregon and Idaho Telegraph Co., in 1866. He joined Asahel Bush in 1869 to form the Salem Ladd and Bush Bank, and was treasurer of the Oregon City

Woolen Mill, 1870. He controlled the Portland Flouring Mills, helped incorporate the Portland and Willamette Railway Co., in 1885, built the Portland Hotel in 1887, besides owning outright three large farms and being partner with Simeon G. Reed in five others where the most advanced cultivation and stock-breeding programs were supported. Oregon lost one of her true builders with his death on Jan. 6, 1893.

**JOSEPH LANE (1801-1881)** was born in North Carolina, lived in Indiana until 1848 and was elected a State Senator, served with the Indiana Volunteers in the Mexican War from which he emerged a Major-General. He came to Oregon in 1849 as Territorial Governor, helped negotiate the 1851 agreement with the Rogue River Indians, was Territorial Delegate, 1851-1859, and U.S. Senator 1859-1861. His presence on the pro-South, pro-slavery Breckenridge-Lane ticket in 1860 ended his political career in Oregon. He lived on his farm near Roseburg until his death on April 19, 1881.

**RICHARD H. LANSDALE (1811-1898)** was born in Maryland, grew up in Ohio where he attended the Medical College of Cincinnati, and practiced medicine until 1834. There followed many restless years that saw him in Indiana until 1841, in Troy, Ohio, thence to Maumee City, Ohio, 1843-1846: to Illinois, 1846-1847, and a member of the Missouri Mounted Volunteers, 1847-1848. He came to Oregon in 1849 by way of California. After a few months at Lafayette he bought 160 acres across the Columbia River on which he platted Vancouver. The failure of this venture freed him for the enthusiastic promotion of Whidbey Island where he founded Oak Harbor, Crescent Harbor, and Coveland, 1852. He served as Indian Agent, 1854-1860, Clerk of the Circuit Court at The Dalles, 1862, and spent 1864-1867 in Washington, D.C. negotiating a $10,000 settlement with the U.S. Government; and finishing at the University of the City of New York Medical College. He returned to practice medicine in Dayton, Oregon, 1867-1869; at Tacoma, W.T., 1869; among the Snohomish Indians, 1873-1876; in Olympia, W.T. 1876-1879, and at the Quinault Indian Agency until his retirement in 1880. He died April 19, 1898.

**DAVIS LAYTON (1822-1862)** was born in Ohio, arrived in Oregon in 1848, and took up a donation claim in Linn County, 1851. He was chosen Captain, Co. H, First Regiment, OMV, Oct. 17, 1855-May 15, 1856. He joined the Oregon Mounted Rangers, May 15, 1856, was chosen as Major, June 2, 1856; and served until Aug. 21, 1856. He was Sheriff of Linn County from 1860 until his unexpected death, Apr. 22, 1862.

**AMOS L. LOVEJOY (1808-1882)** was born in Groton, Mass., worked in a Boston store about 1824 before finishing his education at Cambridge, Mass., and Amherst. He completed his law studies and practiced in Sparta, Missouri before coming to Oregon, 1843, where he enjoyed immediate success in law, business and politics. He sold his share of the Portland townsite to Benjamin Stark in 1845, who joined W. W. Chapman, Stephen Coffin and Daniel Lownsdale in developing and promoting the platted property. Lovejoy was elected to the Territorial House 1846-1850, to the Council 1851-1852 and the House, 1856. He remained an important figure in Oregon's legal, political and civic affairs until his death, Sept. 11, 1882.

**DANIEL H. LOWNSDALE (1803-1862)** was born in Kentucky, lived in Indiana, was in business in Georgia until 1842, and traveled in Europe before emigrating to Oregon in 1845 where he was elected to the Provisional Legislature the next year. He owned Portland's first tannery in which he made the $5,000 worth of leather traded to Francis Pettygrove, Sept. 22, 1848, for the 640 acre townsite of Portland. The following year he sold a half interest in the property to Stephen Coffin, and both of them sold a part interest to W. W. Chapman, Dec., 1849. Lownsdale was president of the Portland and Valley Plank Road Co., chartered in 1851. He was Regimental Quartermaster, First Regiment, OMV, during the Yakima War, 1855-1856. Death cut short his life a few years after the war, May 4, 1862.

**DUGALD MACTAVISH (1817-1871)** followed a normal path of promotion in his career with the Hudson's Bay Company. He began as an apprentice clerk, 1832-1835, at Moose Factory on Hudson Bay: next, he was stationed at Michipicoten, 1835-1837, on the shore of Lake Superior: whence he went to Lachine, 1837-1839, before his years at Fort Vancouver, 1839-1847. The year of the Whitman Massacre, 1847, he was assigned to the Sandwich Islands, from which he returned in 1852 in time to settle at Fort Vancouver, 1853-1858: Fort Victoria, 1858-1859, 1860-1863, and finally brought to Montreal from 1865 until his death May 24, 1871.

**MAURICE MALONEY (    ?-1872)** was born in Ireland, emigrated to the United States where he enlisted in the U.S. Army, Nov. 5, 1836.

158

He was cited and brevetted twice during the Mexican War: at Molino del Rey, Sept. 8, 1847, and at Chapultepec, Sept. 13, 1847. Later, at the siege of Vicksburg, July 4, 1863: and on March 13, 1865 he received additional citations. He retired from the Army, Dec. 15, 1870, and died Jan. 8, 1872.

**CHARLES HENRY MASON (1829-1859)** was born in Fort Washington, Maryland, graduated from Brown University in 1850, admitted to the Rhode Island bar the following year, and appointed Secretary of Washington Territory, 1853. This popular official served as acting-Governor during four extended absences of Gov. Isaac I. Stevens: March 26-December 1, 1854; May 12, 1855-January 19, 1856; August-September, 1857; and August, 1858-July, 1859. After a brief but painful illness of three days, he died at Olympia, July 29, 1859.

**HENRY MATTICE (    ?-1855)** was born in Brown, N.Y., moved to California in 1852, but finally settled in Olympia, W.T. where he prospered sufficiently as a merchant, investor and real estate promoter to have left a moderate estate when he was killed c. Sept. 30, 1855 on the trail through the Cascade Mountains.

**GEORGE W. MAXWELL (1832-1914)** was born in Dayton, Ohio, lived in Indiana until 1840, and in Iowa before coming to Dayton, Oregon in 1851. He spent these first years working in almost every Pacific slope mining camp, but did settle in Cowlitz County, W.T. after serving in the OMV, 1855-1856. He lived here permanently, except for a brief stay in Spokane Falls, W.T., and became a prominent horse breeder. He was elected to the Washington Territorial Legislature, 1872. But ranching filled his life until he retired to Vancouver, Washington, 1906, where he died May 30, 1914.

**JAMES McAULIFF (1828-1906)** was born in Malta, came to Canada with his parents in 1836, and enlisted in the U.S. Army, 2nd Infantry, 1845, in time to fight in the Mexican War, 1846-1848. Later as a member of the U.S. 4th Infantry he was stationed in Michigan in 1848; California, 1852, and discharged at Ft. Vancouver, W.T., 1855. He went into business immediately at The Dalles where he was twice Treasurer of Wasco County before moving to Walla Walla in 1859. There he was County Treasurer, 1862-1867: a member of the Territorial Legislature, 1864: Sheriff, 1869: and eleven times Mayor of Walla Walla before 1882. He died in 1906.

**JOHN McBEAN (c. 1840-1896)** was probably born at the Hudson's Bay Company's Ft. Babine in central British Columbia (then New Caledonia) while his father, William McBean, was Chief Trader. He was a messenger, guide and interpreter in the Yakima War; and worked as a herder Apr.-Aug., 1856, when Col. George Wright was parading through the Yakima country. McBean was an interpreter for General O. O. Howard during his pursuit of Chief Joseph and the Nez Perce, 1877. He performed a like service on the Umatilla Reservation for almost 20 years before being found dead near his home, Aug. 26, 1896.

**WILLIAM McBEAN (c. 1806-1892)** was probably born in Wisconsin and began working for the Hudson's Bay Co. in his late teens when he filled a minor position at Ft. Alexandria (on the Assiniboine River) in 1825. He was Chief Trader at Ft. Babine, 1836-1842, before succeeding Archibald McKinley at Ft. Walla Walla, 1845, where he was Chief Trader from 1847 until his retirement in 1851. He lived on his donation claim in the Frenchtown precinct about two miles from the Whitman Mission site, until his death, April 10, 1892.

**MORTON M. McCARVER (1807-1875)** was born in Kentucky, lived in Illinois, founded Burlington, Iowa, 1834: and was commissary general of Iowa before emigrating to Oregon in 1843. He was instrumental in establishing Linnton, Oregon, 1843-1844: founding Sacramento, California, 1849: and Tacoma, Washington, 1868. This remarkable man was Speaker of the Executive Committee government, 1844-1845, that preceded Provisional Government in Oregon, and a member of the California Constitutional Convention, 1849. He was commisary general of Oregon, 1855-1856. His business interests ranged from a donation claim near Oregon City, 1845, to real estate in Sacramento, 1849-1850: mercantile stores in The Dalles, Auburn, and Idaho City, 1862; selling quartz mines in New York, 1864; speculating in war claims, 1866; and developing a new city on Commencement Bay, Tacoma, Washington, 1868. Complications from a cold contracted while inspecting newly-discovered coal deposits on the upper Puyallup River brought death, April 17, 1875.

**GEORGE B. McCLELLAN (1826-1885)** was born in Philadelphia, appointed to West Point in 1842 and graduated in time to serve in the Mexican War, 1846-1848. He failed to discover a possible railroad route across the Cascade Mountains in 1853, as a member of Isaac I.

Steven's expedition, and resigned his commission four years later. He held successive positions on the Illinois Central Railroad and the Ohio and Mississippi Railroad until Apr. 23, 1861, when he accepted a commission as Major-General in the Ohio Volunteers. Ten days later, May 3, he was given identical rank in the U.S. Army, and began his controversial tour as Chief of Staff and, later, Commander of the Army of Virginia that terminated with his removal by President Lincoln in 1862. Two years later he was the unsuccessful candidate on the Democratic ticket opposing Lincoln. Two years abroad, 1867-1869, preceded his term as Chief Engineer of the New York City Department of Docks, His final public service was as Governor of New Jersey, 1878-1881, a scant four years prior to his death, Oct. 29, 1885.

**JOHN McCRACKEN (1826-1915)** was born in London, England, came to East Haddam, Conn., in 1832, where he attended school until 1843. He clerked in a Fiskeville, R.I. store for three years before moving to New York City. The prospect of profitable mercantile and freighting business lured him to California in 1849. He reached Oregon by Nov., 1850: was Chief Clerk of the Territorial House, 1853, and was appointed by Gov. George Curry as Asst. Quartermaster General, OMV, following A. Zieber's resignation, Jan. 30, 1856. Besides this post he was U.S. Marshal, Oct. 1, 1855-1861. Many years later, 1891, 1895 and 1901, he sat in the State Legislature. He was a commission merchant in Portland and San Francisco until John McCracken & Co., builders supplies, became a recognized Portland firm. He died, Feb. 15, 1915.

**WILLIAM C. McKAY (1824-1893)** was born at Astoria, studied medicine in New York and Ohio, 1838-1842, before he opened a mercantile business at Oregon City, 1843. A short bout with California gold fever, 1849, preceded his building a trading post at the juncture of the Umatilla River and McKay Creek. His business flourished during 1851-1855 until the Indians were alienated by his prominent role in the negotiation of the Treaty of Walla Walla, June, 1855. His subsequent service in the Yakima War, Oct., 1855-May, 1856, furnished the excuse for the natives pillaging and destroying his store and farm. He devoted himself to medicine, for the most part, after the war: first as agency physician at Warm Springs, 1861-1886, as well as in private practice on the Umatilla Reservation, 1868, until his death, Jan. 2, 1893.

**JOSEPH L. MEEK (1810-1875)** was born in Virginia, worked for the American Fur Co. until 1840 when he settled near Hillsboro, Oregon. He assumed a prominent part in the Champoeg meeting, 1843, that organized a provisional government for Oregon. He was elected Sheriff, took a formal census of Oregon in 1845: was chosen for the Provisional Legislature in 1846, 1847: sought additional Federal protection, and returned from Washington, D.C. in 1849 as Oregon's first U.S. Marshal. He served more than ten months in the Yakima War, 1855-1856, usually as a messenger or guide. He spent the remainder of his life living quietly on his farm until death came, June 20, 1875.

**TOUSSAINT MESPLIE (1824-1895)** Roman Catholic priest, born in Belpech, France, March 17, 1824, accompanied Archbishop Francis N. Blanchet to Oregon, Aug. 19, 1847. He was ordained a priest, May 25, 1850, in St. Paul, Oregon: and assigned to St. Peter's Church, The Dalles, 1851-1863. This gregarious, ebullient, kind, tireless priest worked successfully with the Columbia River tribes, the soldiers during the war years, and the permanent settlers. The mineral rush into Idaho, 1862, brought Mesplie's transfer to the new gold fields in 1863. He worked among Indians, soldiers, and white settlers in this entire area until 1882. He was commissioned a U.S. Army chaplain, 1872, after twenty-two years as a volunteer, unpaid chaplain at Ft. Dalles, Ft. Boise, and other posts. He returned from Europe in 1883, after visiting his family for the first time in thirty-six years, only to be court martialed for over staying his leave and was dismissed from the service, Jan. 15, 1884. He spent his declining years with a nephew in Grass Valley, California, until his death, Nov. 20, 1895.

**JOHN F. MILLER (1824-1899)** was born in Kentucky, fought in the Mexican War, 1846-1848, and emigrated to Oregon in 1851. He was elected to the Territorial Legislature, 1853, failed as Democratic candidate for Governor, 1862, but was a delegate to the 1884 Democratic National Convention that nominated Grover Cleveland. Closer to the local scene, he was Quartermaster General during the Yakima War, 1855-1856; Indian Agent for the Grand Ronde Reservation, 1856-1862, and fought against the Modoc Indians in 1873. His 11,000 acre Klamath County ranch demanded most of his attention until he moved to Salem in 1898, where he died, Jan. 25, 1899.

**LYMAN B. MUNSON (c. 1826-1884)** was born in Great Barrington, Mass., came to California in 1849, and was a carpenter on the original building crew at Port Orford, Oregon, in June, 1851. He was elected Captain, Co. I, Benton County, First Regiment, OMV, Oct. 24, 1855-Feb. 29, 1856: and was a staff member under Col. John Kelsey, Second Regiment, OMV, May 3-July, 1856, against the southern Oregon Indians. The greater portion of his life, however, was spent in Boise City, Idaho where he was a revered pioneer until his death, Apr. 6, 1884.

**WILLIAM H. H. MYERS (1830-1914)** was born in Missouri and came to Oregon by way of California in 1852. He taught school after his first planting on Sauvie Island was washed out by high water. He fought in the Rogue River Indian War, 1854: and went looking for Colville gold early enough in 1855 to be back for service against the Yakimas in Co. D, Washington County, First Regiment, OMV, Oct. 1855-May 1856. When the fighting ended, he visited Missouri until 1859: then went looking for gold in Idaho and Oregon, 1860-1863. He settled down to farming and stock raising near Gaston, Ore., 1865-1882, until moving to Forest Grove to spend the last 30 years of his life that ended, Feb. 6, 1914.

**JAMES WILLIS NESMITH (1820-1885)** was born in New Brunswick and twice orphaned at the age of six. His youth was spent in sporadic schooling, voracious reading, and sustained self-improvement before arriving in Oregon, 1843. He shared in organizing the provisional government under which he was a Supreme Court Justice, 1845-1846, and a member of the Legislature, 1846. He took part in the Cayuse War, 1848; that against the Rogue River Indians, 1853; and resigned as Colonel of the 1st Regiment, Oregon Mounted Volunteers, Dec. 4, 1855, probably because of the uselessness of chasing the Yakima Indians in the middle of winter. He was Superintendent of Indian Affairs for Oregon and Washington, 1857-1859: U.S. Senator from Oregon, 1861-1865, and U.S. Representative, 1873-1875. The last ten years of his life were spent on his farm near Derry, Oregon, where he died on June 17, 1885.

**JOHN F. NOBLE (    ?-1899)** was born in Pennsylvania, came to Ft. Vancouver as a civilian clerk in the Quartermaster department in 1849. He was a partner with George C. Bomford and Lloyd Brooke in trading and farming ventures, 1854-1855, on the Whitman Mission site and on their own claims along the Touchet River. After the Yakima War he was employed at Ft. Dalles and Ft. Vancouver, usually as an Agent for the Quartermaster and occasionally as a Sub-Indian Agent until the Civil War saw him serve in the First Oregon Volunteer Cavalry at Ft. Vancouver, Camp Watson, and Ft. Walla Walla until Oct. 20, 1866. He spent four years, 1870-1874, as a clerk in different San Francisco offices; yet, in his declining years described himself as "a gentleman farmer" in Cumberland County, Pennsylvania, where he died in 1899.

**PETER SKENE OGDEN (1794-1854)** was born in Quebec, grew up in Montreal, and became a clerk for the North West Company in 1811. He spent almost his entire adult life in the Far West: along the Columbia River in 1818, in the Shuswap and Thompson River areas of New Caledonia, 1820: at Spokane House in 1823, and as Commander of the Hudson's Bay Company Snake River Brigades, 1824-1829. He sought furs in California during 1829-1830, and along the coast of New Caledonia in 1831-1834, then in the vicinity of Stuart Lake from 1835 to 1844, and at Ft. Vancouver for the closing years, 1845-1851. The last months of his life were spent in Montreal where he died, Sept. 27, 1854.

**CYRUS OLNEY (c. 1815-1870)** was born in Ohio, served four years as Circuit Judge in Iowa, and came to Salem in 1851. He was a member of the Territorial Supreme Court, 1853-1857: a delegate to the State Constitutional Convention, 1857, and served in the Oregon House in 1866 and 1870. He moved to the Sandwich Islands for a time: but returned to Astoria where he died, Dec. 21, 1870.

**NATHAN OLNEY (c. 1829-1866)** was born in Rhode Island, arrived in Oregon in 1845, opened a store at The Dalles, 1847, and captained the volunteer forces fighting the Cayuse Indians, 1848. He reopened his store, 1850, after a passing touch of California gold fever. He operated the DesChutes River ferry and raised cattle, 1853-1864. During these same years he held a variety of public posts: Justice of the Peace, 1854: Deputy Sheriff, 1855: Indian Sub-Agent, guide, and interpreter, 1855-1857; and, City Marshal of The Dalles, 1864. Complication from an old arrow wound brought death, Sept. 15, 1866.

164

**ROBERT M. PAINTER (1827-1868)** was born in Missouri, arrived in Oregon in 1850, and filed on a donation claim in Washington County, 1851. He served in Co. D, First Regiment, OMV, Oct. 15, 1855-May 5, 1856. He married Ella Zieber, Feb. 28, 1859, who became an untimely widow with five small children by his death at Forest Grove, Nov. 3, 1868.

**WILLIAM CHARLES PAINTER (1830-1900)** was born in Missouri, came to Oregon in 1850 where he settled on a donation claim two years later. After his service in Co. D, Washington County, First Regiment, OMV, during the Yakima War, he led a varied life. He worked in the Idaho mines, 1861-1862; was a clerk at Wallula, 1863-1867, and finally settled in Walla Walla where he held a series of public offices. He was Deputy Collector of Internal Revenue, 1868-1871; Receiver in the U.S. Land Office, 1876-1878; and Auditor of Walla Walla County, 1878-1888. He spent the next ten years managing his 1500 acre ranch on Eureka Flat near Walla Walla. He remained partially active until the time immediately preceding his death, Dec. 4, 1900.

**JOEL PALMER (1810-1881)** was born in Elizabeth, Ontario, of American parents, lived in New York, Pennsylvania, and Indiana before coming to Oregon, 1847. He was Superintendent of Indian Affairs in his first year: and, a second time, in the critical years, 1853-1856. He was Speaker of the House as well as Major-General of the Oregon Militia, 1862. He was a member of the State Senate in 1864, 1865 and 1866. His business interests included the platting of Dayton, Oregon, on part of his donation claim: the incorporating of the Columbia River Rail Road Co., 1862: and control of a toll road right-of-way from Hood River to Troutdale with ferries at Hood River and Sandy. This latter asset was a key purchase when the Oregon Railroad and Navigation Co. was formed in 1879. He died at his Dayton home, June 9, 1881.

**CHARLES MARIE PANDOSY (1826-1891)** was born in Marseilles, France, joined the Roman Catholic missionary group of the Oblates of Mary Immaculate, came to Ft. Walla Walla where he was ordained a priest, Jan. 2, 1848. He worked among the Yakimas until the 1855-1856 war closed the mission. He established a new mission at Anse du Sable, on the east shore of Lake Okanagan, B.C., 1859. Here he lived and labored for more than 30 years until he died, Feb. 6, 1891.

**FRANCIS W. PETTYGROVE (1812-1887)** was born in Maine, came to Oregon City by way of Honolulu in 1843, opened a general store, traded for furs, built a grain warehouse at Champoeg, and bought 320 acres adjacent to the site of Portland. All of his assets in Oregon City, Champoeg, and Portland (a rumored $75,000) were sold and the money plunged into Benicia, California real estate in 1849. This venture was a disaster, as was a $10,000 investment in Oregon City property made upon his return in 1850. Whatever was salvaged he took with him to Port Townsend, W.T. in 1851, where he filed on a donation claim April 24, 1852. He was the new settlement's first postmaster, 1852-1856, and long-time Superintendent of Schools, 1857-1875. His last years were lived in retirement until his death on Oct. 5, 1887.

**CHARLES B. PILLOW (1822-1860)** a jeweler and watchmaker, was elected Recorder for Portland in 1852, and a member of the Board of Councilmen, 1853. He served in Co. A, First Regiment, OMV, Oct. 13, 1855-May 15, 1856; and in Co. A, Battalion of Mounted Rangers, OMV, May 17-Aug. 21, 1856. He died in Portland, Sept. 12, 1860.

**HENRY L. PITTOCK (1836-1919)** was born in London, England, brought to the United States when three years old, attended school in Pennsylvania, and learned the printer's trade from his father. When he came to Oregon in 1853, he was hired as a typesetter by Thomas J. Dryer, owner of the *Weekly Oregonian*. Seven years later Pittock acquired control of the paper for unpaid wages. A daily edition appeared in 1861 as proof of the new owner's enterprise. *The Daily Oregonian* flourished through the years while it increased Pittock's stature, power, and wealth until his death on Jan. 28, 1919.

**GABRIEL JAMES RAINS (1803-1881)** was born in North Carolina, graduated from the U.S. Military Academy in 1827, and began his service on the frontier. He fought in the Seminole War, 1836-1842, and took part in other actions that were customary duty for the Army in pre-Civil War times. He resigned July 31, 1861 to accept an appointment as Brigadier General in the Confederate Torpedo Bureau, June 1864. He died Aug. 6, 1881.

**NARCISSE RAYMOND (c. 1817-    )** was born in Canada, worked for the Hudson's Bay Co., until retiring with his Indian wife and children to the Walla Walla Valley where he filed on a donation claim, Sept. 15, 1853. He was in charge of Brooke, Bomford and Company's stock at Waiilatpu at the time of the 1855 Indian fighting. He died prior to June 22, 1887, according to documents filed with the U.S. Court of Claims.

**SIMON GANNETT REED (1830-1895)** was born in Massachusetts, came to Portland in 1852 where he worked for W.S. Ladd & Co. The company name was Ladd, Reed & Co. before long as a preliminary to his giant step forward when he joined with Ainsworth, Kamm, Ladd, Thompson and others in forming the Oregon Steam Navigation Co., 1860, an incredibly lucrative Columbia River freight forwarding monopoly. He and Wm Ladd had interests in the Oregon Telegraph Co., 1852, and the Oregon Central Railroad, 1866, together with extensive scientifically operated farms and ranches. Reed purchased control of the Bunker Hill and Sullivan silver mine in Idaho's Coeur d'Alene Mountains in 1887; a very profitable operation whose control he had relinquished to California and New York interests by 1891. He died in Pasadena, California, Nov. 7, 1895.

**PASCAL RICARD (1805-1862)** was born in Allauch, near Marseilles, France. He was ordained a Roman Catholic priest in 1831, joined the missionary group of the Oblates of Mary Immaculate, and came to the Oregon country in 1847. His ten years on the frontier were taken up with his founding St. Rose's Mission (the passing predecessor of St. Joseph's Mission) among the Yakimas, 1847. A year later, June, 1848, he established St. Joseph's Mission four miles south of New Market (which became Tumwater, W.T.) on Puget Sound. He returned to France in June, 1857, where he died at Notre Dames des Lumieres, Jan. 9, 1862.

**CYRUS K. RIGGS (1834-1856)** came to Oregon from Illinois in 1844. He served in Co. G, Polk County, First Regiment, OMV, as a Private until appointed Quartermaster & Commissary, First Sergeant, at Ft. Henrietta, Jan. 31, 1856. He was dead less than a year later, Dec. 21, 1856, from a wound received Sept. 19, 1856, while serving in Co. K, Washington Territorial Volunteers.

**ANTOINE RIVAIS (c. 1816-1886)** was one of the early settlers on French Prairie in the Willamette Valley: his name being on the first tax roll for Oregon, that of 1844. He served as Captain, Co. K, Marion County, First Regiment, OMV, after Narcisse Cornoyer's election as Major, March 7, 1856. Rivais (or, Rivet) lived in Portland for two years after the Yakima War, 1856-1858; whence he moved to Ravalli, Montana on the Flathead Indian Reservation where he died, Feb. 23, 1886.

**ALVIN B. ROBERTS (1832-1922)** was born in Ohio and came to Portland where the stone-cutting firm of Roberts and Hartle was established. He served in Co. A, Multnomah County, First Regiment, OMV, Oct. 13-Dec. 19, 1855. Later he went back to stone-cutting in Boise City and Walla Walla. His donation claim included part of Walla Walla's townsite. He achieved local fame for opening a pioneer nursery on his land in 1860. He returned to Portland before his long life ended, Jan. 2, 1922.

**PETER LOUIS NAPOLEON ST. ONGE. (1842-1901)** Roman Catholic priest, born in St. Cesaire, P.Q., Apr. 14, 1842, studied in St. Hyacinth Seminary, P.Q., before coming to Vancouver, W.T., Oct. 15, 1864. Here he studied and taught at Holy Angels College until Bishop A.M.A. Blanchet ordained him a priest, May 31, 1866. He overcame the bishop's reluctance and was assigned to St. Joseph Mission, Ahtanum, Sept. 1867, to rebuild what the Oregon Mounted Volunteers burned down in Nov., 1855. His physical labors were impeded by a serious back injury; but not his intellectual study of the Yakima language published as, *Alphabet Yakama Contenant Les prieres, les cantiques, et le Catechisme dans la meme langue. A l'usage des enfants de la Tribu des Yakamas, sous le patronage des R.R.P.P. Jesuites*. Montreal: Imprime de la Providence: 1872. He left the mission in June, 1871, to return to the Diocese of Albany, N.Y. Glens Falls, Albany, and the vicinity, henceforth, was the scene of his pain ridden labors before retirement and death at St. Hyacinth, P.Q., Nov. 26, 1901.

**ANDERSON H. SALE (c. 1829-1898)** served in Co. F, Marion County, First Regiment, OMV, Oct. 15, 1855-Feb. 16, 1856. He was assigned the special duty of guarding and transporting the remains of Capt. Charles Bennett after his slaying in the Battle of Walla Walla, Dec. 7-10, 1855. Sale transferred to Co. A, Recruiting Battalion, Capt. E. J. Harding, cmdg., in which he served from Feb. 16-May 3, 1856: and was Regimental Sergeant Major, March 8-May 3, 1856. He settled in Clatsop County after the war and played a minor part in civic affairs during the many years before his death, Nov. 28, 1898.

168

**VALENTINE W. SCHAEFFER (1828-1892)** was born in Dayton, Ohio, grew up in Cass County, Illinois, and came to Oregon, 1852. He fought in the Rogue River War as a member of the Ninth Regiment, OMV, Aug.-Sept., 1853, and served in Co. A, First Regiment, OMV, Oct. 13, 1855-May 5, 1856, in the Yakima War. After returning to Cass County, 1857, he married, settled down on his farm where he stayed, except for service in the Civil War, until death, Jan. 9, 1892.

**JOHN SETTLE (c. 1824-1862)** settled near Lebanon, Oregon in 1846, and served as Captain, Co. D, Recruiting Battalion, OMV, Feb. 1-May 26, 1856. He moved to Steilacoom, W.T. after the war, whence he left for the Idaho mines in 1862. He became separated from his nephew James while traveling in Idaho and no trace of John was ever found.

**R. W. SHAW (1827-     )** was born in New York, lived in Ohio, and practiced medicine at Salem, Oregon, 1855-1860. Although Asst. Surgeon General of the OMV, 1855-1856, he retained his practice in Salem until moving to Dayton, Ore., after the war, where he was still practicing in 1862.

**PHILIP HENRY SHERIDAN (1831-1888)** was born in New York, graduated from West Point in 1853, and served along the Rio Grande River before his assignment to the Pacific Northwest, 1855-1856. His fame rests especially upon his devastation of the Shenandoah Valley at a critical time in the Civil War, Sept.-Oct. 1864. The post-war years saw him Military Governor of Louisiana and Texas, 1867: Commander of the Military Division of Missouri, 1869: a corresponding office in the Western and Southwestern Military Divison, 1878: and finally, Commander-in-Chief of the Army from 1884 until his death, June 1, 1888, at Nonquitt, Mass., two weeks after finishing his *Memoirs*.

**GEORGE K. SHIEL (1825-1893)** was born in Ireland, grew up in New Orleans, and was admitted to the bar in Ohio prior to his arrival in Oregon, 1854. He practiced law in Salem, did his stint in the OMV during the Yakima War, 1855-1856, before his successful campaign on the Democratic ticket for the 37th U.S. Congress in which he sat from July 30, 1861-March 3, 1863. His refusal to take the oath of allegiance, and his consequent disbarment, embittered the last 30 years of his life. He lived in retirement at Salem until his accidental death, Dec. 12, 1893.

**JAMES SINCLAIR (1806-1856)** was born at Oxford House, a Hudson's Bay Company post between Lake Winnipeg and Hudson Bay. He was educated in the Orkney Islands and Edinburgh, 1819-1826. He worked for the HBC one year, 1826-1827, to satisfy his indenture. He became a free trader at the Red River Settlement and was so sympathetic to the metis unrest by 1838 that the Company was anxious to facilitate his departure. He was retained to lead a party of 116 people to the Company farms on the Cowlitz and Nisqually Rivers in the Oregon Country, 1841. He returned to Red River for four years, 1842-1846, of further trade and agitation that climaxed with his dispatch to London as an advocate for the metis, 1846-1847. He spent the years, 1848-1852, mostly traveling in Illinois, Missouri, California, Oregon and back to New York by way of Panama and Cuba. He led another party of 100 that reached Ft. Walla Walla Dec. 16, 1854. He had an unusual agreement with the Company permitting him to engage in private lumbering and stock raising, plus a salary of 150 pounds per annum, while he filled the role of Chief Trader at Ft. Walla Walla. Upon the expiration of his five year contract that began June 1, 1853, the physical facilities of the Fort would belong to him. He had assumed management of Ft. Walla Walla on Jan. 16, 1855; a short year before its destruction in the intense fighting, Dec., 1855; and a scant four months prior to his own death in the Cascades Massacre, March 26, 1856.

**ALONZO A. SKINNER (1814-1877)** was born in Ohio, admitted to the bar in 1840, and served as Prosecuting Attorney in Putnam County, Ohio, 1842-1845. The thirty years following his arrival in Oregon in 1845 witnessed his service in a number of public posts. He was Circuit Judge under the Provisional Government, 1846; Indian Agent in the Rogue River Valley, 1851-1853; Clerk of Lane County, 1862-1864; and Collector of Customs at Coos Bay, 1870-1877. He died Apr. 30, 1877, not long after moving to Santa Barbara, California.

**THOMAS A. SMALL (1834-1900)** was born in Tennessee, emigrated to Oregon in 1852, remained long enough to serve during the Yakima War in Co. K, Marion County, First Regiment, OMV, Oct. 30, 1855-May 31, 1856, before returning to Tennessee the next year. He lived there until 1860 then, after traveling extensively through the South, he settled in Otterville, Missouri, 1864. Here he completed 14 years as Marshal, three terms as Deputy Sheriff, and one as County

Clerk. He was assistant to the warden of the Missouri State Penitentiary, Jefferson City, at the time of his death, Feb. 7, 1900.

**SIDNEY A. SMITH (1824-1901)** was born in Vermont, studied medicine in Boston, lived in Illinois, remained briefly in California in 1851 before coming to Oregon the next year where he filed on a donation claim, 1853. His medical practice in Albany, Peoria and Halsey, Oregon, extended over an impressive 47 years before his 1899 retirement. He died in Portland two years later, Nov. 14, 1901.

**WILLIAM GREGORY SMITH ( ?-1877)** succeeded Archibald Barclay as Secretary of the Hudson's Bay Company, Feb. 12, 1855: a post retained until Jan. 1871, when William Armit became Secretary and Smith continued as Consulting Secretary until his death prior to Oct., 1877.

**HERMAN H. SNOW (1828-1886)** born in Ohio, was Absalom J. Hembree's son-in-law, by reason of his marriage to Nancy Matilda Hembree, Oct. 7, 1853. He died in Renton, W.T., Apr. 20, 1886.

**HENRY HARMON SPALDING (1803-1874)** accompanied Marcus Whitman to the Oregon mission in 1836 and began working at Lapwai, on the Clearwater River, among the Nez Perce Indians. He spent 38 years at Lapwai, Ft. Vancouver, Brownville, Ore., before going back to Lapwai to die, Aug. 3, 1874.

**BENJAMIN STARK (1820-1898)** was born in New Orleans, came to Oregon in 1845 where he engaged in trade with the Sandwich Islands and bought A. L. Lovejoy's interest in the site of Portland. A brief try for California gold, 1848, preceded the study of law that led to his admission to the bar in 1851. He was elected to the Oregon Territorial Legislature, 1852-1853, to the State Legislature in 1860, and as U.S. Senator from Oregon, 1861-1862. He retired to New London, Conn., at the outbreak of the Civil War and remained there until his death, Oct. 10, 1898.

**LINTON STARR (c. 1832- )** served in Co. I, Benton County, First Regiment, OMV, Oct. 24, 1855-Feb. 29, 1856.

**JAMES B. STEPHENS (1806-1889)** was born in Brooke County, Virginia (later West Virginia), worked as a cooper in Indiana and Ohio before buying a farm in Illinois. His first years in Oregon,

171

1844-1847, were spent making barrels for the meat and flour trade of the Hudson's Bay Company. He carved his niche in Oregon history with his vigorous real estate promotions that began in 1850 with East Portland, and continued through many projects, some controversial, that were uniformly profitable until his death, March 22, 1889.

**ISAAC I. STEVENS (1818-1862)** was born in Massachusetts, graduated from West Point, 1839, and served mostly with the U.S. Army Engineers, 1839-1853, except for service on General Winfield Scott's staff in the Mexican War, 1846-1847. He was appointed Governor of Washington Territory, Superintendent of Indian Affairs, and Chief of the Pacific Railroad Survey in 1853, after resigning from the U.S. Army. He remained Governor until his election as Territorial Delegate in 1857. He was commissioned Colonel, New York 79th Highlanders, soon after the Civil War began in 1860, and was killed in action near Fairfax Courthouse, Sept. 1, 1862.

**WILLIAM D. STILLWELL (1824-1921)** was born in Ohio, crossed the plains from Missouri to Oregon which he reached in 1845 after stopping at Henry H. Spalding's Lapwai Mission in 1844 and at Whitman's Waiilatpu Mission, 1845. He fought the Cayuse Indians in 1848, looked for California gold the next year, and finally filed on a donation claim in Yamhill County, 1851. He was in Co. C, Recruiting Battalion, First Regiment, OMV, Capt. A. P. Ankeny, cmdg., Jan. 29-May 15, 1856. Nine years later he became identified with the development of the Tillamook area, after moving there to care for his aging father. He was elected Sheriff, 1872, Superintendent of Schools, 1874, County Assessor, 1888, and a State Representative, 1891. He had financial interests in the Tillamook Lumbering Company, the Stillwell Addition to Tillamook, and other local enterprises. When this revered pioneer died, June 19, 1921, he had been a successful farmer, investor, real estate promoter and civic office holder.

**ROBERT R. THOMPSON (1820-1908)** was born in Pennsylvania, and lived in Ohio before coming to Oregon, 1846. When he returned to The Dalles, 1850, after successfully seeking California gold, Orlando Humason and Thompson developed a very lucrative monopoly of upper Columbia River freighting and transportation. Their ships, wagons and portage roads merged with the Oregon Steam Navigation Co., 1860, to constitute an even more powerful and profitable combine for the fortunate owners. The entire complex was sold to Henry Villard's expanding transportation empire in 1879. Thompson lived on until March 10, 1908, as an immensely wealthy investor and developer in Portland and San Francisco.

**VICTOR TREVITT (1827-1883)** was born in New Hampshire, came to Oregon in 1847 where he worked a short time as a printer's devil for the Salem *Oregon Statesman*, before settling at The Dalles. He ran the Mt. Hood Saloon, was a partner in a freighting business, and played a prominent role in civic affairs. He was Chief Clerk of the State Senate in 1854, elected a Representative in 1858, and was back in the Senate, 1868, 1870. Failing health induced him to move to San Francisco in 1882, where he died, Jan. 27, 1883.

**AMOS UNDERWOOD (1834-1917)** was born in Cincinnati, came to Oregon in 1852, worked on the riverboats, and after his service against the Yakimas, 1855-1856, farmed for many years near Underwood, W.T. and Hood River, Oregon, where he died, Dec. 16, 1917.

**HENRY DAVIES WALLEN (    ?-1886)** was born in Georgia, and appointed to West Point from Florida, Sept. 1, 1836. His military career advanced along the usual route from 2nd Lieutenant, 4th Infantry, Oct. 4, 1840; to Major, 7th Infantry, Nov. 25, 1861, and Colonel, 2nd Infantry, by Feb. 19, 1873. He retired a year later, Feb. 18, 1874, but lived until Dec. 2, 1886.

**MARCUS WHITMAN (1802-1847)** was born in Rushville, N.Y. where he began studying medicine at the age of 21. He graduated from medical college in Fairfield, N.Y., 1832, and set up his practice in Wheeler, N.Y. Three years later he accompanied Samuel Parker to the Oregon Country and established a mission at Waiilatpu in the Walla Walla Valley, 1836. His very success in farming at this Oregon Trail landmark and his inability to stem a smallpox epidemic among the Indians were significant incitements to his murder, that of his wife, and twelve others, Nov. 29, 1847, by the Cayuse Indians.

**HIRAM WILBER (1818-    )** was appointed first City Marshal of Portland, April 14, 1851. He served in Co. D, First Regiment, OMV, Oct. 17, 1855-May 15, 1856: he was Captain (replacing Thomas

173

R. Cornelius) from Jan. 28-May 15, 1856: and of Co. B, Oregon Mounted Rangers, May 15, 1856-Aug. 21, 1856.

**ALFRED V. WILSON (1826-1859)** was born in Tennessee, came to Oregon in 1850, where he settled a donation claim in Yamhill County, 1853. He worked in the pre-war years, 1854-1855 as a messenger for Wells, Fargo & Co. He was Captain, Co. A, First Regiment, OMV, Oct. 13, 1855-May 15, 1856: and of Co. A, Battalion of Mounted Rangers, OMV, May 15-Aug. 21, 1856. He died suddenly in Portland, June 27, 1859.

**JOHN WITHERS (    ?-1892)** was born in Tennessee, entered West Point from Mississippi, July 1, 1844: and was commissioned a 2nd Lieutenant, 4th Infantry, Jan. 31, 1850. He was Regimental Quartermaster, 1853-1856, which included his tour at Fort Vancouver, W.T. He resigned his commission in order to serve as a Colonel, Asst. Adjutant General in the Army of the Confederate States, 1861-1865. He lived for nearly 30 years after the Civil War and died on Feb. 3, 1892.

**THOMAS A. WOOD (1838-1904)** was born in Montgomery, Illinois, reached Portland, Nov., 1852: served in the OMV against the Yakimas, 1855-1856, and was prominent in subsequent efforts to collect war claims from the U.S. Government. He was an energetic promoter as his turpentine factory, 1863-1873, a grist mill at La-Grande, Oregon, 1864, and his presence in impressive real estate projects, 1878, fully attest. Events completely vindicated his foresight in platting 320 acres into Sellwood (a Portland suburb) in 1883, and by buying 538 acres southwest of Portland as early as 1889. He died on the site of his successes, Sept. 27, 1904.

**JOHN ELLIS WOOL (1784-1869)** was born in New Burgh, N.Y., attended country school and educated himself in Troy, N.Y., until he was commissioned a Captain in the U.S. Army, 1812. His rise was rapid as he became Inspector-General of the Army and a Colonel, Apr. 29, 1816. The next 47 years saw him in varied roles as he advanced in rank and responsibility. He was raised to Brigadier-General, 1841, commanded the Eastern Military Division, 1848-1853, the Department of the Pacific, 1854-1857, and returned to command the Department of the East, 1857. He was promoted to Major-General, May 16, 1862, more than a year before he retired on Aug. 1, 1863; six years before his death, Nov. 10, 1869.

**GEORGE WRIGHT (1803-1865)** was born in Norwich, Vermont, graduated from West Point in 1822 to begin a long and varied career in the U.S. Army. He served in Wisconsin, 1822-1824: Missouri, 1826-1828, and along the border during the Canadian disturbances, 1837-1838. He fought in the Seminole War, 1840-1842: the Mexican War, 1846-1847, and came to Ft. Vancouver in 1856. After his 1858 campaign against the Spokane and neighboring tribes, he was given command of the Department of Oregon, 1861, and assumed command of the Department of the Pacific, Sept. 28, 1861. He was at sea en route to his new command of the Department of the Columbia when the *Brother Jonathan* sank off Crescent City, California, July 30, 1865. He and his wife were buried in State House Square, Sacramento, California, Oct. 22, 1865.

# Map of the campaign

November, 1855—May, 1856.

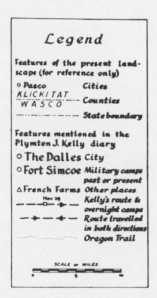

# Bibliography

## Manuscript sources

The notes make clear the character and wide dispersal of the manuscript sources used in editing and elucidating the Kelly diary. Specific documents cited in the notes are not listed again in this section. Here attention is directed toward the less ordinary types of material consulted.

Thomas Cornelius' letters in the Huntington Library, San Marino, California are marked with unusual candor, unconcealed personal color, and highly individualistic spelling. The "Regimental Order Book First Regt of Oregon Mounted Volunteers Thomas R. Cornelius Col. Commndg Regt. Wm H. Farrar Adjutant of Regiment" preserved in the Northwest Collection, Public Library, Spokane, Washington, supplied much precise data for the clear understanding of the diary.

It is tedious, fascinating, and satisfying to uncover biographical minutiae about generally obscure people. The task would be unthinkable without the Indian War Pension Papers, the Biographical file, the Oregon Pioneer file, the Scrapbooks, and the Vital Statistics file in the exceptionally rich collections of the Oregon Historical Center, Portland. These must be supplemented by the notably helpful Oregon Territorial Papers, Oregon Provisional Government Papers, and other official records administered by the Oregon State Archives, Salem. The present study is obviously indebted to the official Muster Rolls of the Oregon Mounted Volunteers and related documents kept in the Adjutant General's office, Salem.

The many other original sources consulted were no less helpful because their nature was more familiar.

178

# Printed sources

AITKEN, MICKEY, "Story of Clinton Kelly and the Schools," *Sunday Oregonian*, Sept. 19, 1948.

*Albany City Directory, Embracing a Resident and Business Directory for 1878* (Albany, Mansfield & Monteith, 1878).

ALLEY, B. F. and J. P. MUNRO-FRASER, *History of Clark County, Washington Territory, Compiled from the Most Authentic Sources* (Portland, The Washington Publishing Company, 1885).

BAILEY, WALTER, "The Barlow Road," *OHQ*, 13 (1912).

BAIN, READ, "Educational Plans and Efforts by Methodists in Oregon to 1860," *OHQ*, 21 (1920).

BANCROFT, HUBERT H., *History of Oregon, 1848-1888* (*The Works of Hubert Howe Bancroft*, v. 30) (San Francisco, The History Company, 1888).

BARTH, GUNTER, ed., *All Quiet on the Yamhill, The Civil War in Oregon, The Journal of Corporal Royal A. Bensell, Company D, Fourth California Infantry* (Eugene, University of Oregon Press, 1959).

BISCHOFF, WM. N., *The Jesuits in Old Oregon 1840-1940: A Sketch of Jesuit Activities in the Pacific Northwest.* (Caldwell, Caxton, 1945).

———, "The Yakima Campaign of 1856," *Mid-America*, 31 (1949).

BRADLEY, CYPRIAN, and EDWARD KELLY, *History of the Diocese of Boise.* (Caldwell, Caxton, 1953).

BREWSTER, WM. L., *William Mead Ladd of Portland Oregon* (Portland, Metropolitan Press, 1933).

*British and American Joint Commission on Hudson's Bay and Puget's Sound Agricultural Companies' Claims. In the Matter of the Hudson's Bay Company. Testimony on the Part of the United States. Part Second* (Washington City, McGill & Winthrow, 1867).

BURCH, CAROLINE F., "The Burch Family," *Polk County Pioneer Sketches*, 2 (1929).

CAMPBELL, JAMES M., "The Campbell Family," *idem.*

CAREY, CHAS. H., *A General History of Oregon Prior to 1861*, 2 vols. (Portland, Metropolitan Press, 1936).

———, *The Oregon Constitution and Proceedings and Debates of the Constitutional Convention of 1857* (Salem, State Printing Department, 1926).

———, *History of Oregon*, 3 vols. (Chicago, Pioneer Publishing Co., 1922).

CARTWRIGHT, C. M., "Glimpses of Early Days in Oregon," *OHQ*, 4 (1903).

CHAMBERS, EDITH K., *Genealogical Narrative, A History of Three Pioneer Families, The Kerns, Popes, and Gibsons* (Eugene [Privately Printed] 1943).

CLEVELAND, ALFRED A., "Social and Economic History of Astoria," *OHQ*, 4 (1903).

CLINE, GLORIA G., *Peter Skene Ogden and the Hudson's Bay Company.* (Norman, University of Oklahoma Press, 1963).

COAN, C. F., "Federal Indian Relations of the Pacific Northwest," *OHQ*, 22 (1921).

COMAN, EDWIN T., and HELEN M. GIBBS, *Time, Tide and Timber A Century of Pope & Talbot* (Stanford, Stanford University Press, 1949).

CORNING, HOWARD M., ed., *Dictionary of Oregon History* (Portland, Binfords & Mort, 1956).

*Correspondence and Official Proceedings Relating to the Expeditions Against the Indians* (Salem, Asahel Bush, Territorial Printer, 1855).

CRANDALL, LULU D., "Indian Fighters, Settlers in Wasco County," *OHQ*, 31 (1930).

DART, RICHARD, "Settlement of Green Lake County," *Proceedings of the State Historical Society of Wisconsin, 1909* (Madison, The Society, 1910).

[DISTURNELL, W. C.] *Disturnell's Business Directory and Gazetteer of the West Coast of North America* (San Francisco, W. C. Disturnell, 1882).

DONALDSON, THOMAS, *Idaho of Yesterday* (Caldwell, Idaho, Caxton Printers, Ltd., 1941).

DOUGLAS, JESSE S., "Jefferson Institute, 1857-99," *OHQ*, 33 (1932).

DRURY, CLIFFORD M., *Marcus Whitman, M.D. Pioneer and Martyr* (Caldwell, Idaho, Caxton Printers, Ltd., 1937).

———, *Marcus and Narcissa Whitman & the Opening of Old Oregon*, 2 vols. (Glendale, A. H. Clark, 1973).

ELLIOTT, T. C., "The Chinook Wind," *OHQ*, 33 (1932).

———, "The Dalles-Celilo Portage: Its History and Influence," *OHQ*, 16 (1915).

———, "The Murder of Peu-Peu-Mox-Mox," *OHQ*, 35 (1934).

———, "Peter Skene Ogden, Fur Trader," *OHQ*, 11 (1910).

EVANS, ELWOOD, *History of the Pacific Northwest: Oregon and Washington*, 2 vols. (Portland, North Pacific History Co., 1889).

Farrar, Victor J., ed., "Diary of Colonel and Mrs. I. N. Ebey," *WHQ*, 7 (1916); 8 (1917).

Fleming, R. Harvey, ed., *Minutes of Council, Northern Department of Rupert Land, 1821-1831* (Toronto, The Champlain Society, 1940).

Frazer, Robert W., ed., *Mansfield on the Condition of the Western Forts 1853-1854.* (Norman, University of Oklahoma Press, 1963).

———, *Forts of the West, Forts and Praesidios and Posts, commonly called Forts West of the Mississippi River to 1898.* (Norman, University of Oklahoma Press, 1965).

Garth, Thos. R., "Archeological Excavations at Fort Walla Walla," *PNQ*, 43 (1952).

———, "The Archeological Excavation of Waiilatpu Mission," *OHQ*, 49 (1948).

Gaston, Joseph, *The Centennial History of Oregon 1811-1912,* 4 vols. (Chicago, S. J. Clarke Publishing Co., 1912).

———, *Portland Oregon, Its History and Builders in Connection with the Antecedent Explorations, Discoveries, and Movements of the Pioneers that Selected the Site for the Great City of the Pacific,* 3 vols. (Chicago, S. J. Clarke Publishing Co., 1911).

*Genealogical Material in Oregon, Donation Land Claim Records,* 4 vols. (Portland, Genealogical Forum of Portland, Oregon, 1953-1962).

Gilbert Frank T., *Historic Sketches of Walla Walla, Whitman, Columbia, and Garfield Counties, Washington Territory and Umatilla County, Oregon* (Portland, A. G. Walling, 1882).

Gill, Frank B., "Oregon's First Railway," *OHQ*, 25 (1924).

Gillette, P. W., "A Brief History of the Oregon Steam Navigation Company," *OHQ*, 5 (1904).

Grant, Frederic James, *History of Seattle, Washington* (New York, American Publishing and Engraving Co., 1891).

Guie, H. Dean, *Bugles in the Valley, Garnett's Fort Simcoe* (Yakima, The Author, 1956).

Hafen, LeRoy R., "Mountain Men — William Craig," *The Colorado Magazine,* 11 (1934).

Haller, T. N., "Life and Public Services of Colonel Granville O. Haller, Citizen and Pioneer," *The Washington Historian,* 1 (1900).

*The Hargrove Correspondence, 1821-1843,* G. P. de T. Glazebrook, ed. (Toronto, The Champlain Society, 1938).

Hawthorne, Julian, *The Story of Oregon,* 2 vols. (New York, American Historical Publishing Co., 1892).

HEITMAN, FRANCIS B., *Historical Register and Dictionary of the United States Army*, 2 vols. (Washington, D.C., Government Printing Office, 1903).

HIMES, GEORGE H., "History of the Press of Oregon 1839-1850," *OHQ*, 3 (1902).

HINES, H. K., *An Illustrated History of the State of Washington* (Chicago, Lewis Publishing Co., 1893).

*History of Southern Oregon Comprising Jackson, Josephine, Douglas, Curry and Coos Counties* (Portland, A. G. Walling, 1884).

*History of the Bench and Bar of Oregon* (Portland, Historical Publishing Co., 1910).

HODGKIN, FRANK E., and J. J. GALVIN, *Pen Pictures of Representative Men of Oregon* (Portland, Farmer and Dairyman Publishing House, 1882).

HOOPES, ALBAN W., *Indian Affairs and Their Administration with Special Reference to the Far West 1849-1860* (Philadelphia, University of Pennsylvania Press, 1932).

HOUCK, LOUIS, *A History of Missouri From the Earliest Explorations and Settlements Until the Admission of the State into the Union*, 3 vols. (Chicago, R. R. Donnelly & Sons Co., 1908).

IDLEMAN, H. L., "Long Continued Influences of Methodism in Oregon," *OHQ*, 43 (1942).

*An Illustrated History of Klickitat, Yakima, and Kittitas Counties with an Outline of the Early History of the State of Washington* ([n.p.], Interstate Publishing Co., 1904).

JOHANNSEN, ROBERT W., "The Oregon Legislature of 1868 and the Fourteenth Amendment," *OHQ*, 51 (1950).

*Journal of the Council of the Legislative Assembly of the Territory of Oregon: During the Seventh Regular Session from Dec. 3, 1855 to Jan. 31, 1856. The Eightieth Year of the Independence of the United States.* (Salem, Asahel Bush, Territorial Printer, 1856).

*Journal of the House of Representatives of the Territory of Oregon: During the Seventh Regular Session, from Dec. 3, 1855 to Jan. 31, 1856* (Salem, Asahel Bush, Territorial Printer, 1856).

*Journal of the Proceedings of the Council of the Legislative Assembly of the Territory of Oregon, During the Regular Session, from Dec. 1, 1856 to Jan. 29, 1857* (Salem, Asahel Bush, Territorial Printer, 1857).

KAPPLER, CHARLES, J., ed., *Indian Affairs: Laws and Treaties*, 4 vols. (Washington, D.C., Government Printing Office, 1904-1929).

KELLY, LAURA, and ESTHER KELLY WATSON, *The Kelly Family*, 2 Parts (Portland, [privately printed], 1973).

KELLY, RICHMOND, *The Kelly Clan* (Portland, privately printed, 1901).

KNUTH, PRISCILLA, *"Picturesque" Frontier: The Army's Fort Dalles.* [Portland, Oregon Historical Society, 1966-1967].

KRAYBILL, D. B., "Colonel William Craig Mountain Man and First Permanent Settler in Idaho," *West Virginia History,* 19 (1958).

LANG, H. O., ed., *History of the Willamette Valley, Being a Description of the Valley and its Resources, with an Account of its Discovery and Settlement by White Men, and its Subsequent History, Together with Personal Reminiscences of its Early Pioneers* (Portland, Himes & Lang, 1885).

LARSELL, O., *The Doctor in Oregon, A Medical History* (Portland, Oregon Historical Society, 1947).

LENT, D. GENEVA, *West of the Mountains, James Sinclair and the Hudson's Bay Company* (Seattle, University of Washington Press, 1963).

LOCKLEY, FRED, "Reminiscences of Colonel Ernst Dosch," *OHQ,* 25 (1924).

LOMAX ALFRED L., "Oregon City Woolen Mill," *OHQ,* 32 (1931).

———, "Pioneer Woolen Mills of Oregon," *OHQ,* 30 (1929).

LORD, ELIZABETH, *Reminiscences of Eastern Oregon* (Portland, Irwin-Hodson Co., 1903).

MCARTHUR, HARRIET K., "Biographical Sketch of Hon. J. W. Nesmith," *Transactions of the Oregon Pioneer Association, 1886.*

MCARTHUR, LEWIS A., *Oregon Geographic Names* (Portland, Binfords & Mort, 1952).

MACDUFFEE, K. M., "Navigation Upper Willamette River 1846-1936," Typescript (Portland, U.S. Engineer Office, 1940).

[MCLOUGHLIN, JOHN] *The Letters of John McLoughlin from Fort Vancouver to the Governor and Committee. Second Series. 1839-1844.* E. E. Rich, ed. (London, Hudson's Bay Record Society, 1943).

MCNEAL, WILLIAM H., *History of Wasco County Oregon* [The Dalles, The Author, 1952].

MEANY, EDMOND S., "Captain William Hale Fauntleroy; A Neglected Character in Northwestern History," *WHQ,* 18 (1927).

———, ed., "Waman C. Hembree Yakima Indian War Diary," *WHQ,* 16 (1925).

———, "Morton Mathew McCarver, Frontier City Builder," *Annual Report of the American Historical Association 1909* (Washington, D.C., Government Printing Office, 1911).

MILES, CHARLES and O. B. SPERLIN, eds., *Building a State, Washington, 1889-1939* (Tacoma, Washington State Historical Society, 1940).

MILLER, EMMA GENE, *Clatsop County, Oregon, A History* (Portland, Binfords & Mort, 1958).

MILLS, RANDALL V., *Stern Wheelers Up Columbia; A Century of Steamboating in the Oregon Country* (Palo Alto, Pacific Books, 1947).

MUNSON, MYRON A., *The Munson Record. A Genealogical and Biographical Account of Captain Thomas Munson and His Descendants*, 2 vols. (New Haven, The Munson Association, 1895).

NELSON, HERBERT B., and PRESTON E. ONSTAD, eds., *A Webfoot Volunteer: The Diary of William M. Hilleary, 1864-1866* (Corvallis, Oregon State University Press, 1965).

NICHOLS, M. LEONA, *The Mantle of Elias: The Story of Fathers Blanchet and Demers in Early Oregon* (Portland, Binfords & Mort, 1941).

*Official Army Register of the Volunteer Force of the United States Army for the Years 1861, '63, '65*, Part VII (Washington, D.C., Adjutant General's Office, 1867).

OLIPHANT, J. ORIN, ed., "Journals of the Indian War 1855-56," [Journal of Robert M. Painter and Journal of William C. Painter] *WHQ*, 15 (1924).

OLIVER E. H., ed., *The Canadian North-west Its Early Development and Legislative Records Minutes of the Red River Colony and the Northern Department of Rupert's Land*, 2 vols. (Ottawa, Government Printing Bureau, 1914).

ORCUTT ADA M., *Tillamook: Land of Many Waters* (Portland, Binfords & Mort, 1951).

[OREGON STATE OF], *Biennial Report of the Secretary of State — Oregon — 1897-98* (Salem, W. H. Leeds, 1899).

OWEN HOMER L., "Nesmith: Pioneer Judge, Legislator, Farmer, Soldier, Senator, and Congressman," *Reed College Bulletin*, 28 (1950).

[PARSONS, WILLIAM and W. S. SHIACH], *An Illustrated History of Umatilla County and of Morrow County with a Brief Outline of the Early History of the State of Oregon* ([Chicago], W. H. Lever, 1902).

*Polk County Centennial Souvenir Booklet and Program* (Dallas, Oregon, The Centennial Committee, 1947).

*The Portland Directory, for the Year Commencing January, 1866: Embracing a General Directory of Residents, and a Business Directory* ... (Portland, S. J. McCormick, 1866) The first Portland directory appeared in 1863 and has continued under different publishers' auspices to the present. These were of manifest assistance in tracing certain people linked to the Plympton Kelly diary.

*Portrait and Biographical Record of Portland and Vicinity Oregon* (Chicago, Chapman Publishing Co., 1903).

*Portrait and Biographical Record of Western Oregon* (Chicago, Chapman Publishing Co., 1904).

*Portrait and Biographical Record of the Willamette Valley Oregon* (Chicago, Chapman Publishing Co., 1903).

PRATT, HARRY E., ed., "22 Letters of David Logan, Pioneer Oregon Lawyer," *OHQ*, 44 (1943).

PROSCH CHARLES, comp., "Biographical Sketch of General Isaac I. Stevens." *Transactions of the Washington Pioneer Association for the Years 1883 to 1889, Inclusive.*

PROSCH, THOMAS W., *McCarver and Tacoma* (Seattle, Lowman & Hanford, 1906).

REED, HENRY E., ed., "Lovejoy's Own Story," *OHQ*, 31 (1930).

REESE, J. W., "OMV's Fort Henrietta: on Winter Duty, 1855-56," *OHQ*, 66 (1965).

RINEHART, W. V., "War in the Great Northwest," *WHQ*, 22 (1931).

ROBERTS A. B., "The Yakima War of 1855: The Compaign [sic] to Walla Walla; The Capture of the Most Noted War Chief of the Pacific Coast; A Chapter from the Reminiscences of a Pioneer," *Clark County History*, 8 (1967).

ROCKWOOD, E. RUTH, ed., "Diary of Reverend G. H. Atkinson," *OHQ*, 41 (1940).

ROEHM, MARJORIE CATLIN, *The Letters of George Catlin and His Family.* (Berkeley, University of California Press, 1966).

SALE, A. H., "Indian War Recollections," *Oregon Native Son*, 1 (1899-1900).

SANDERS, GEORGE B., comp., *Members of the Legislature, State of Oregon, 1860-1949* (Salem, State Library, 1949).

SANDERS, WILMA K., comp., *Members of the Legislature of Oregon, 1843-1967* (Salem, Oregon State Library, 1968).

SARGENT, ALICE Applegate, "A Sketch of the Rogue River Valley and Southern Oregon History," *OHQ*, 22 (1921).

SCHOLL, LOUIS, "Recollections of Sixty Years," *Walla Walla Up-to-the-Times*, 26 (1908).

SCOTT HARVEY W., *History of the Oregon Country*, 6 vols. (Cambridge, Mass., The Riverside Press, 1924).

———, *History of Portland, Oregon with Illustrations and Biographical Sketches of Prominent Citizens and Pioneers* (Syracuse, N.Y., D. Mason & Co., 1890).

SCOTT, LESLIE M., "History of the Narrow Gauge Railroad in the Willamette Valley," *OHQ*, 20 (1919).

SCOTT, LESLIE M., "Soil Repair Lessons in the Willamette Valley," *OHQ*, 18 (1917).

SHELLER, ROSCOE, *The Name Was Olney* (Yakima, Franklin Press, 1965).

SMITH, ALICE ELIZABETH, *James Duane Doty Frontier Promoter.* (Madison, State Historical Society of Wisconsin, 1954).

SPAID, STANLEY SHELDON, "Joel Palmer and Indian Affairs in Oregon" (Unpublished Ph.D. Dissertation, University of Oregon, 1950).

STEVENS, HAZARD, *The Life of Isaac Ingalls Stevens*, 2 vols. (Boston, Houghton, Mifflin and Co., 1900).

STURGIS, CYRUS C., "William C. McKay," *Walla Walla Union Bulletin*, Oct. 9, 1949.

SWAN, JAMES G., *The Northwest Coast* (Fairfield, Washington, Ye Galleon Press, 1966).

"Territorial Governors of Idaho," *Idaho Yesterdays*, 7 (1963).

THEODORE, SISTER MARY, *Heralds of Christ the King: Missionary Record of the North Pacific, 1837-1878.* (New York, P. J. Kenedy & Sons, 1939).

THIAN, RAPHAEL P., *Notes Illustrating the Military Geography of the United States, 1813-1880* (Washington, D.C., Government Printing Office, 1881).

THOMPSON, ERWIN N., *Whitman Mission National Historic Site* (Washington, D.C., Government Printing Office, 1964).

———, *Shallow Grave at Waiilatpu: the Sagers' West* (Portland, Oregon Historical Society, 1969).

THROCKMORTON, ARTHUR L., *Oregon Argonauts: Merchant Adventurers on the Western Frontier* (Portland, Oregon Historical Society, 1961).

TOBIE, HARVEY E., *No Man Like Joe. The Life and Times of Joseph L. Meek.* (Portland, Binfords & Mort, 1949).

TURNBULL, GEORGE S., *History of Oregon Newspapers* (Portland, Binfords & Mort, 1939).

UNDERWOOD, AMOS "Mr. Amos Underwood's Story of the Capture and Death of Peu-Peu-Mox-Mox," *Ladd & Bush Quarterly*, 2 (1914).

United States Department of the Interior, *Biographical and Historical Index of American Indians and Persons Involved in Indian Affairs*, 8 vols. (Boston, G. K. Hall & Co., 1966).

———, *Report of the Secretary of the Treasury on the State of the Finances for the Year Ending June 30, 1863* (Washington, D.C., Government Printing Office, 1863).

VESTAL, STANLEY, *Joe Meek: The Merry Mountain Man* (Caldwell, Idaho, The Caxton Printers, Ltd., 1952).

186

VICTOR, FRANCES F., *The Early Indian Wars of Oregon, Compiled from the Oregon Archives and Other Original Sources. With Muster Rolls.* (Salem, F. C. Baker, 1894).

————, "The First Oregon Cavalry," *OHQ*, 3 (1902).

*Wasco County Directory Alphabetical and Classified. Together with the Portland Business Directory, 1895* (Portland, Portland Directory Co., 1895).

WEISEL, GEORGE F., *Men and Trade on the Northwest Frontier as Shown by the Fort Owen Ledger* (Missoula, Montana State University Press, 1955).

WEST, OSWALD, "Reminiscences and Anecdotes: The Harding Brothers," *OHQ*, 52 (1951).

WILLIAMS, GEORGE H., "Political History of Oregon from 1853 to 1865," *OHQ*, 2 (1901).

WOODWARD, WALTER C., *The Rise and Early History of Political Parties in Oregon, 1843-1868* (Portland, J. K. Gill, 1913).

YOUNG, FREDERIC G., "Portland's Canyon Road," *OHQ*, 19 (1918).

# Newspapers

A notable lack of collected biographical data inspired a dogged search in contemporary and subsequent newspapers for some information on nearly all of the men active in the narrative. There remained a few that foiled all efforts to identify them with greater precision. The notes make clear that certain publications were especially fruitful in this quest, while many others contributed to the cumulative fund of knowledge. The Oregon newspapers, understandably, were especially beneficial. *Portland Weekly Oregonian,* and its successor, *Daily Oregonian, Portland Oregon Weekly Times,* and *Salem Oregon Statesman* supplied much material. Smaller publications were good sources for news of the outlying areas, e.g., *State Rights Democrat* (Albany, Oregon), *Daily Mountaineer* (The Dalles), *East Oregonian* (Pendleton), and *Pendleton Tribune*. Some who moved to neighboring regions may be followed in the *Idaho Democrat* (Boise), the *Pioneer and Democrat* (Olympia, W.T.), the *Washington Standard* (Olympia), or the *Walla Walla Union Bulletin*.

# Index

188

189

This book was designed by Nurmi Hansen and printed by Craftsman Press, Seattle. The type for the text is ten point Melior; for the heads, Corral. The stock is Antique Offset Book. The cover cloth is Milbank Linen M 4647.